MW00775445

A Practical Guide
for
Effective Biblical Counseling

WAYNE MACK

A Practical Guide
for
Effective Biblical
Counseling

Utilizing the 8 "I"s
to Promote True Biblical Change

Wisdom is so very precious. The wisdom Wayne Mack gained through over fifty years of studying, ministering the Scriptures to hurting people, and discipling me and so many others to use God's Word effectively is priceless. I thank the Lord that this wisdom has been passed on to countless others through the pages of this book. Read it carefully and repeatedly. You will be blessed.

DR. MARSHALL ASHER, MABC, ACBC:
Co-author of *The Christian's Guide to Psychological Terms*

Although this book is packed with vital truth for the caring of souls in a more biblical and effective way, it is presented in simple and manageable portions. This is a reading every local church, biblical counseling institution, Christian university, and Christian high school should utilize to both introduce others to the call/field of biblical counseling, but also to equip the saints to better minister God's grace to others in need. Undoubtedly, the book's greatest feature is its continual focusing others toward the sufficiency of Christ and His Word. I highly recommend Dr. Mack's book, which I believe is a timeless gift to the church.

DANIEL R. BERGER II, MS, MA, PhD:
Pastor, Faith Fellowship Church, Clarence, NY; Founder/Director of Alethia International Ministries; Director, Faith Biblical Counseling Center; Professor of Biblical Counseling

The godly wisdom Wayne Mack has acquired through more than fifty years of preaching, teaching, and counseling are on full display in this marvelous book. His masterful exposition of the eight "I"s make this book a must-read for biblical counselors and all who desire to enhance their ability to apply God's Word to their lives, as well as to the lives of others. I highly recommend this book.

JOHN BLACKBURN:
Elder, Providence Church, Duluth, GA

A Practical Guide for Effective Biblical Counseling: Utilizing the 8 "I"s to Promote True Biblical Change will make you a more effective biblical counselor—whether you are just getting started or are already a seasoned veteran. Dr. Wayne Mack, writing from a wealth of biblical study and extensive counseling experience, has given us an essential field guide to the complex terrain of biblical counseling. Dr. Mack's eight foundational principles, the eight "I's," function as fixed reference points that enable the counselor to keep his bearings and to stay on course as he seeks to help the counselee deal with his problems and grow in Christlikeness. Read it; reread it; refer back to it often, and you and your counselees will be better for it.

TY BLACKBURN:
Pastor, Providence Church, Duluth, Georgia

Dr. Wayne Mack has served God's people well. He has worked tirelessly over decades to provide the church with reliable biblical resources. His insights as an author and his experience as a biblical counselor can be clearly seen in *A Practical Guide for Effective Biblical Counseling: Utilizing the 8 "I"s to Promote True Biblical Change*. The privilege of teaching biblical counseling to students in Africa cannot be done effectively without his work.

The task of counseling and discipleship can be overwhelming at times. The counseling method presented in this book is made up of eight parts masterfully organised to form a comprehensive process of discipleship. It will not only equip pastors and lay people to interpret the complexities of human problems but also help them identify and present the applicable God-directed solutions to those problems.

SYBRAND DE SWARDT:
Pastor, Lynnwood Baptist Church, Pretoria, South Africa;
Director, Strengthening Ministries Training, ABD Southern Seminary

It was my privilege to be Dr. Mack's student in 2004 as he taught the eight "I"s at Master's University. God used this very instruction to crystallize my understanding of the counselor's role in ministry to others. Even better, I now had confidence in the Lord to know where to start in counseling others, and the direction in which counseling could be most effective. Through these principles, I was taught how, with the Holy Spirit's help, to be a compassionate, helpful friend to fellow strugglers in this fallen world. I cannot recommend this book highly enough.

TERRY DEVITT:
Elder/Counseling Director, The Bible Church of Owasso, Owasso, OK

Dr. Mack is a gift to the church. His thorough treatment of issues related to biblical counseling cannot be overstated. By God's grace, he continues to provide rich biblical instruction, enabling biblical counselors to be more effective. It has been my rare privilege to sit under the teaching of Dr. Mack, then to teach these very materials to others, and now gladly endorse this book.

In his latest work, he gives us a book that will help counselors be more fruitful servants in God's hands. He speaks not only to the importance of the content of our counsel but also to how we are to counsel.

The eight "I"s, beginning with *Involvement* and ending with *Integration*, are spiritual gold in the counseling setting. They are indeed practical guides for effective counseling to benefit both counselor and counselee. Read it, and you will be a more effective counselor, able to minister to the broken and hurting of this world, to the glory of Christ.

DR. GLENN DUNN:
Pastor/Teacher, Cornerstone Bible Fellowship; Moderator of FIRE; Director of the Biblical Counseling Institute; ACBC Certified Counselor

The ministry of counseling others as a church member or as a designated counselor or pastor is a daunting task. We need help from those who go before us. Wayne Mack had three remarkable teachers who expertly guided him: the Holy Spirit, the Bible, and his own vast experience. We can learn from a man who has such tutors. In this short work, we have a compact counselor's guide to lovingly and biblically direct those we help into a fulfilling walk with God. Keep this tool close by and refer to it often.

JIM ELLIFF:
President, Christian Communicators Worldwide; A founding pastor of Christ Fellowship of Kansas City

I have the highest regard for Dr. Mack, an esteemed man of God who is committed to the sufficiency of Scripture. As one of the founding fathers of the biblical counseling movement, he is a treasure and his teaching is priceless. A biblical counselor *par excellence*, Dr. Mack is the man from whom you want to learn the methodology of biblical counseling. His eight "I"s help give structure to the counseling process as we strive to help others become more like Jesus. *A Practical Guide for Effective Biblical Counseling* is a must-read for any biblical counselor, whether you are a novice or a seasoned counselor.

BARBARA ENTER, MABC:
Conference Speaker; Co-Author of *Who Needs A Friend When You Can Make A Disciple?*

In Galatians 6:1, the apostle Paul writes to the church and says, "Brethren, even if anyone is caught in any trespass, you who are spiritual restore such a one. . . ." In His kindness, several years ago the Lord used Dr. Mack's teaching on the eight "I"s to edify and equip me to understand how to biblically restore a brother caught living outside of God's will. I wholeheartedly commend Dr. Mack's book, *A Practical Guide for Effective Biblical Counseling,* as a biblically sound and practical tool in restoring brothers and sisters who find themselves "caught in trespasses" in word or deed.

PAUL HAMLINE:
Pastor of Missions & Biblical Counseling, The Bible Church of Little Rock

As a young convert, I encountered the eight "I"s and the rest of Dr. Mack's teaching on biblical discipleship very early in my Christian walk. It has not only shaped my relationship with Christ but has profoundly shaped and equipped me for the ministry of His Word. The eight "I"s is not only a method that applies to formal counselling but also gives practical guidance toward building deep and impactful relationships for Christ within the family, church, and workplace. Therefore, this book is not only essential for biblical counselors but also relevant for anyone who will make the effort to read it.

JANNES HATTINGH:
Elder at Lynnwood Baptist Church, Pretoria, South Africa

I had the privilege of studying the eight "I"s under Dr Mack's tutelage shortly after he arrived in South Africa. Anybody who has ever had the pleasure of the thorough instruction in his classes would know that the tools gained would be the heartbeat of the many counselling situations you would face later. Dr. Mack combines his vast experience in applying these principles practically and his passion for helping counselees find meaningful biblical solutions to life issues, by providing a platform on which all serious counselors should build their discipleship and mentoring programs.

The eight "I"s will not only ensure a systematic and exhaustive pattern for you, but will also develop in you the necessary skills required of a faithful biblical counselor who wishes to ensure meaningful change in folks that are hurting!

By applying these principles in my own ministry, I have learned how to be attentive and be a careful listener, exercise patience and humility, show a genuine interest in my counselees while maintaining a non-judgmental and unbiased approach, learn how to ask clarifying questions, and not jump to conclusions. I believe that this book, the latest in Dr. Mack's series of helpful resources for the biblical counseling movement, is a summary of his many years of expertise in helping others—you *will* benefit from this!

NEIL HENRY:
Member of Faculty at Bible Institute of South Africa;
Pastor at Metropolitan Evangelistic Church, Lavender Hill

Wayne Mack offers clear, biblical teaching about change and helps demystify "counseling." He's done this for the nearly fifty years that I've known him. In this book, he shows that change occurs through the process of discipleship. He shows how brothers and sisters have roles in nurturing one another in the likeness to Christ through their practical, down-to-earth (incarnational) caring ministry.

RICK HORNE, D.Min.:

Associate Director, The Urban Ministry Institute (TUMI), Chester, PA & Mid-Africa Liaison for Oakseed International Ministries

Since I've had the privilege to sit under Dr. Mack's instruction in biblical counseling classes over the years, I've already been exposed to the principles set forth in his Eight "I"s of Biblical Counseling. However, until now they haven't appeared in a book as comprehensive as this one. This book offers a step-by-step method for ministering to those who come for help.

Dr. Mack, a spiritual giant, is one of the kindest, most compassionate people I know. It's obvious that he practices what he preaches in this book. These interwoven truths are so important to being able to counsel, parent, and disciple effectively—for the glory of Jesus Christ. I'm delighted to have it in my personal library and will refer to it often.

DEBORAH HOWARD:

Author, Little Rock, AR

For decades, Dr. Mack has produced faithful biblical resources that honor our Lord Jesus, sharpen counselors, and help transform the lives of counselees. In this particular work, Dr. Mack has expanded on his eight "I"s of Biblical Counseling, providing the reader with a standalone resource dedicated to implementing these eight principles in their counseling practice. My personal ministry has benefitted from Dr. Mack's eight "I"s. I'm thankful that this work will be readily available to counselors around the world. I highly recommend Dr. Mack's work to you!

T. DALE JOHNSON JR., PH.D.:

Executive Director, ACBC

Director of Counseling Programs, Midwestern Baptist Theological Seminary

Biblical counseling is rooted in our conviction that as believers, we can confidently apply instruction, encouragement, correction, and guidance from God's Word to all the issues of life. And since Scripture is the very Word of God, it is infinitely more helpful, more trustworthy, and more powerful than any methodology borrowed from secular psychology. After all, God's Word alone is able to discern the thoughts and intentions of our hearts and point us reliably in the direction we should go. No genuine believer should struggle with that truth, but many apparently do. Wayne Mack helped pioneer the biblical counseling movement, and he has long been the most effective, articulate advocate and trainer in the field. Now he has distilled his best insights in book form, and it is an indispensable manual for biblical counselors. Highly recommended.

PHIL JOHNSON:
Executive Director, Grace to You, Valencia, CA

Oh, the wisdom and knowledge of God in gifting Dr. Mack with years of counseling experience to write a book to guide the counselor to greater confidence in counseling. This book discusses both the doctrinal and practical levels of counseling and is a much-needed resource for every biblical counselor to be effective in leading the counselee to greater godliness and righteous living, through the Word of God. Thank you for this inspirational, practical book on how to counsel biblically. It will truly be a tremendous guide to help one another in our knowledge and growth into the image of Christ.

LIZELLE JONKER:
Centre Director/ACBC Counsellor;
Bethany Pregnancy Counselling Care Centre, Centurion, South Africa

As a pastor who performs biblical counseling and equips his church to do the same, nobody's resources have been more beneficial to me than those from Dr. Wayne Mack. He is one of the fathers of biblical counseling and few people have done as much to encourage Christians to look to God's Word for the answers to the problems we face on this side of heaven. This book is a treasure trove of decades of counseling wisdom. Fortunately for us, as long as Dr. Mack draws breath, he continues to want to pass along his knowledge. This book will be a blessed addition to the library of anyone interested in counseling others with the Bible.

SCOTT LAPIERRE:
Senior Pastor, Author, Speaker, Woodland Christian Church, Woodland, WA

This is a wonderfully useful handbook for biblical counselors. No one currently training counselors is better equipped for the task or more firmly anchored in Scripture than Wayne Mack. He writes as he teaches (and as he counsels)—with extraordinary clarity, biblical precision, unapologetic boldness, and deep passion for the truth of God's Word. There is an overabundance of bad counsel and bad counseling methods in the world today. Dr. Mack offers a refreshing and thoroughly edifying antidote.

DR. JOHN MACARTHUR:
Pastor, Grace Community Church, Sun Valley, CA;
Chancellor Emeritus of The Master's University and The Master's Seminary

❖

Is there anything more exciting than being used by God to help someone change? If God has saved you, you want to help others know Jesus and obey Him better. But how? Knowing where to start is often difficult. You need a process to help you. Pick up this book! Read it! And I am convinced God will help you learn to more effectively help others. What could be better than glorifying God by doing that?

JOSH MACK:
Senior Pastor, Cornerstone Bible Church, Orange County, California

As a follower of Christ, a husband, a parent, a pastor, and a missionary-church planter, my goal in life is to see Christ formed in me and those God has put under my shepherding care. To fulfil this task, I need good tools that are well written, concise, clear, and yet packed with biblical truth and wisdom. I need tools that can be used anywhere from devotions in the home, lectures in the seminary classroom, or classes for training tribal church leaders. I need tools that can be used as a quick reference or for personal, in-depth Bible study. Dr. Mack's *A Practical Guide for Effective Biblical Counseling* is just such a tool. In fact, it's not just a good tool, it's an *excellent* tool, and I highly recommend it!

RYAN MITCHELL:
Missionary-Church Planter in Papua New Guinea

We live in a blessed day where there are several writers who are on the same intellectual level of biblical counseling as Jay Adams. Wayne Mack is truly a Jay Adams for our day as he has proven, time and time again, in his vast writings on biblical counseling. This new book takes Mack's writings up to an even higher notch than ever before as fifty years of biblical counseling study and experience combine themselves into his writing. I recommend that this book be read by biblical counselors cover to cover and then kept as a manual for reference for the course of their ministries.

ROBERT NORMAN, M.Th:
Author; Missionary with Straight Up Missions, Romania

This book equips you with the knowledge and skills to inspire and help people change. It also demonstrates a lifelong commitment to instructing, discipling, and helping people change. Dr. Mack brings a rich experience, understanding, and the wisdom of the Scriptures to life in the book. He does this in ways that also help counselor and counselee build a warm and loving relationship. Churches that read the book and apply Dr. Mack's 8 "I"s stand to be strong and effective communities of Christians loving and living in true fellowship.

DR. CHRISTOPHER C. NSHIMBI:
Director, Institute for Strategic and Political Affairs,
University of Pretoria, South Africa

When the topic of biblical counseling comes up, there are only a few prominent names which are virtually synonymous with it. Wayne Mack is one of those names. Dr. Mack has been involved with the national and international influence of biblical counseling for over five decades now and he is still writing, teaching, leading, and championing what both the biblical counseling movement truly is and is not. In his latest book, Mack seeks to explain the practical steps to his approach in actually sitting down with hurting people and counseling them from God's Word. These important steps in helping the hurting are excellent principles—and are themselves coming straight from Scripture itself—and which, when followed, will make you and me more effective counselors of others. If you desire to be a better counselor of those who come to you for answers for their spiritual struggles, read and heed this book from one whose counseling impact has been long felt—far and wide.

DR. LANCE QUINN:
Pastor, Bethany Bible Church, Thousand Oaks, California;
Board Member and Fellow, Association of Certified Biblical Counselors

The church of the Lord Jesus Christ has been commissioned to make disciples and to teach them to observe all of the teachings of Jesus as a disciplined follower in His steps. I have been using the eight principles contained in this book to teach in-depth discipleship for almost three decades. These principles will change your own life and will enable you to effectively teach others how to grow and change and become disciplined followers of Jesus Christ. If you are searching for an in-depth discipling methodology, this is it. I highly recommend Wayne's work to you.

ROBERT B. SOMERVILLE, D.Min:
Adjunct Faculty, The Master's University, Valencia, CA

This book is intended for the careful student of biblical counseling and discipleship! Dr. Wayne Mack is a pioneer and skillful pastoral counselor of biblical counseling with decades of worldwide experience. His book, *A Practical Guide for Effective Biblical Counseling* is loaded with biblical wisdom in how to be a counselor with a comprehensive view of addressing the serious problems of the heart. All counselors should understand the eight "I"s of Biblical Counseling if they are interested in doing an effective job of helping the counselees or disciples to be more Christlike in handling and resolving their problems. In fact, the theological template of the eight "I"s will be an invaluable tool for every counselor as a guide for effective self-assessment and improvement. I can see how it will be used as a training manual for decades to come!

DR. JOHN D. STREET:
Professor, The Master's University and Seminary;
President, ACBC Board of Trustees, Valencia, CA

The title, *A Practical Guide for Effective Biblical Counseling*, says it all. This book is immensely practical, very effective, and truly biblical. Through many years of profiting from Dr. Mack's ministry and writing, those three concepts have always stood out—practical, effective, and biblical. All of us are called to counsel each other (Rom. 15:14) and this book will provide you with the tools you will need to properly do that. Dr. Mack has culminated his life's work in this book by providing us with the eight principles we, as counselors, must follow to be truly effective. If you are a pastor, counselor, or a church member who counsels others, you must get a copy and master it. I wish it had been available when I began in the ministry over sixty years ago.

CURTIS C. THOMAS:
Retired pastor and author, Little Rock, AR

A Practical Guide for Effective Biblical Counseling:
Utilizing the 8 "I"s to Promote True Biblical Change
Dr. Wayne Mack

Copyright © 2021 Shepherd Press

ISBNS:
978-1-63342-249-0 (paper)
978-1-63342-250-6 (ePub)
978-1-63342-251-3 (mobi)

Unless otherwise noted, Scripture quotations are from the ESV®
(The English Standard Version®), copyright © 2001 by Crossway, a
publishing ministry of Good News Publishers. Used by permission. All rights reserved.

No part of this publication may be reproduced, or stored in a
retrieval system, or transmitted, in any form or by any means,
mechanical, electronic, photocopying, recording or otherwise,
without the prior permission of Shepherd Press.

Cover design and typeset by www.greatwriting.org

Printed in the United States of America

Shepherd Press
P.O. Box 24
Wapwallopen, PA 18660
www.shepherdpress.com

COUNSEL FOR THE HEART

A RESOURCE for WORD-BASED TRANSFORMATION and PRACTICAL DISCIPLESHIP

Contents

This book is dedicated to

my mentor and friend,

the father of the biblical counseling movement in America,

Dr. Jay Adams.

Pronouns of Gender

In this book, given that there are many case studies and counseling scenarios, the editing policy is to render gender-indefinite singular pronouns as *he* or *him,* rather than the more pedantic *he or she, him or her,* etc. Readers are respectfully notified that use of the masculine is intended to serve as both masculine and feminine.

Acknowledgments

Thank you, my dear wife, Carol. You have stood with me and encouraged me for sixty-four years in my ministries for Christ and His church. I couldn't have done any of this without your continued love and support. You're truly a wife of noble character, my partner through life.

Eternal thanks to Jay Adams. I believe he would be well pleased with this work. He is the man the Lord used to teach me the basic fundamentals of true biblical counseling over fifty years ago. I give thanks to God for the way He used this man to bring me and hundreds of other Christians to a fuller understanding of and commitment to the sufficiency of Scripture for understanding and solving problems.

Much gratitude and appreciation belong to my friend, John MacArthur. He gave me the opportunity to teach at The Master's University. That opportunity enabled me to continue to hone these principles of biblical counseling and to teach them to hundreds of students.

Thank you, Deborah Howard, for the superb job you did for Christ on this book. You took a mere skeleton of my outline and wrapped a narrative around it, covering my content with muscle and flesh, and turning it into this excellent product. I think this may be one of my most useful books and it wouldn't have been written without you. Carol and I are forever grateful.

I'm so grateful to the many people who contributed such kind endorsements for this book. Thank you for the time and effort it took for you to encourage us by your belief in this project.

Foreword

You hold in your hands an important book by an important man. Dr. Wayne Mack is a patriarch in the biblical counseling movement. For fifty years, he has been training biblical counselors. God has used him to help establish ongoing counseling and equipping ministries in Pennsylvania, California, and South Africa. His books are benefitting Christians around the world. Even though he has been busy teaching and writing, he always finds time to practice biblical counseling. This wasn't merely to keep himself sharp. It is because he and his dear wife, Carol, love people and faithfully care for them—especially in the context of their local church. Wayne's counseling experience informs and enriches every page he writes.

I was first exposed to Dr. Mack's work in the early 1980s, a time when all of the books published by the resurgent biblical counseling movement could fit on one (short) shelf. As a very young pastor serving a diverse congregation in the Middle East, I had full confidence in God's Word to transform lives, but very little practical wisdom or experience. I was so grateful to God for the practical help Wayne's *Homework Manuals* and his book, *Strengthening Your Marriage,* provided for me and my counselees in those early days of ministry.

After we were forced to leave the Middle East in 1987, I took my first formal counseling course at Westminster Seminary in California under George Scipione where I was taught Wayne's Seven "I"s (before the eighth "I" was added). In the early 1990s, my wife, Caroline, and I had the joy and privilege of getting to know Wayne and Carol who remained heroes to us while also becoming dear friends.[1]

Since then, I have had the blessing of building upon the foundation they laid. For several years, I was an adjunct professor at the flourishing biblical counseling program which he established at the The Master's University. Two summers ago, we enjoyed the immense blessing of serving alongside them in South Africa where God has helped them to remain fruitful unto old age (Ps. 92:14).

I was amazed to see the passion, sharpness of mind, and energy of Dr. Mack at an age by which most men would have been retired for twenty years. As we taught together, I was exhausted while Wayne seemed to be just warming up. Like Jesus, Wayne's food is doing the will of the Father (John 4:34). Five years ago, I was inspired by the Macks' example of twice answering the call to leave a comfortable and secure place to serve in a location which offers the greatest opportunity for usefulness in ministry (Ps. 90:12,17) when we moved to Charlotte to build a biblical counseling program at Reformed Theological Seminary.

I believe this is one of the most important books Wayne Mack has written. One of the greatest challenges I face as a professor of biblical counseling is teaching people *how* to counsel using God's Word. The eight "I"s are Dr. Mack's important contribution which answers the *how to do it* question with a scripturally based methodology for biblical counseling. Just as what the Bible teaches about various aspects of doctrine is logically arranged in books of Systematic Theology, Dr. Mack has arranged the various key elements of biblical counseling in a logical and orderly fashion. The eight "I"s are in a sense the crown jewels of Wayne's ministry, polished through more than fifty years of teaching and counseling experience.

---

1   I also learned PEACH then PREACH before PREACHD became the acronym for our data gathering. A later effort to systematize the practice of biblical counseling can be found in Paul Tripp's book, *Instruments in the Redeemer's Hands*, in which he organizes our work in four categories—love, know, speak, and do. Some have noticed that each of Tripp's four categories corresponds to two of Dr. Mack's 8 "I"s.
Love—Involvement, Inspiration
Know—Inventory, Interpretation
Speak—Instruction, Inducement
Do—Implementation, Integration
See *Counseling: How to Counsel Biblically* by Wayne Mack and John MacArthur.

While Dr. Mack has written about the eight "I"s in other places, this is his most comprehensive and refined expression of the core of his teaching. He offers useful case studies. He also gives specific warnings about how people who claim to practice biblical counseling can be guilty of carelessness by failing to gain a personal connection, listen well, and interpret life situations biblically.

When Wayne asked me to write this foreword, he revealed that I was not his first choice. Jay Adams was preferred, but he has recently gone to be with the Lord. Many of the other dear patriarchs of our movement have also left us recently. I am thankful that Dr. Mack remains. The Lord has kept him beyond fourscore years (Ps. 90:10). One reason, in addition to his ongoing work in South Africa, may have been so that he could write this book for all of us.

I urge you to take advantage of the privilege of sitting under a Master Teacher and Counselor by carefully reading this volume. It is saturated with scriptural wisdom. You will find yourself referring back to it for years to come.

Dr. Jim Newheiser
Director of the Christian Counseling Program
Associate Professor of Counseling and Pastoral Theology
Reformed Theological Seminary, Charlotte, North Carolina
Executive Director, IBCD (The Institute for Biblical Counseling and Discipleship)

Introduction

Who will benefit from this book? Anyone involved in counseling troubled people. Who will benefit from this book? Anyone who strives to disciple others for Christ. Who will benefit from this book? Every parent who wants to promote effective communication and faith-building conversations with their children. Who will benefit from this book? Any Christian committed to serving others through the Word of God. Who will benefit from this book? Anyone who wants to live a life pleasing to the Lord, utilizing the principles set forth in Scripture. If you fall into any of these categories, you will benefit from this book.

In a ministry spanning well over fifty years, God has certainly taught me a thing or two about this topic. Rarely surprised, I believe I have encountered just about everything under the sun during those years. My ministry has consisted of preaching, teaching, pastoring, counseling, writing, church planting, and shepherding people. The one thing that qualifies me to write this book, though, is my experience in the arena of biblical counseling.

With Dr. Jay Adams, George Scipione, Pastor William Goode, Dr. Robert Smith, and others, I worked to bring biblical counseling back into Christian churches. We worked tirelessly in our effort to develop the foundation of the biblical counseling movement, and into the development of NANC (National Association of Nouthetic Counselors), which has since become ACBC (Association of Certified Biblical Counselors).

After creating that foundation, we continued to work to build a strong biblical method in the approach to counseling in various areas of ministry. God has since given me the opportunity to continue to labor, tweak, and refine until that method has been honed into its current form.

I had the opportunity to serve at The Master's College in California as a professor of biblical counseling, teaching hundreds of students as part of the curriculum to serve as pastors, worship leaders, missionaries, and counselors. I preached all over the country and taught biblical counseling classes in different venues.

At the age of seventy, my dear wife, Carol, and I moved our ministry to Pretoria, South Africa. By God's grace, He has chosen to use me and others devoted to this cause to bring to the continent of Africa the first schools designed to teach men and women of God the steps to discipleship through biblical counseling. We have brought ACBC there, and these newly trained counselors have gone out into their areas of ministry utilizing what we've taught them through our schools and classes. Biblical counseling is spreading through Africa.

Through all these endeavors, I never stopped counseling and teaching. My classes have taught thousands. And now, as my physical health grows weaker, I find that my spiritual desire to preserve and disperse these essential steps to biblical counseling has grown stronger. My entire ministry has led me to this point. My goal in writing this book is to reach the maximum number of people with these building blocks of effective counseling—and, more than that, to help others live a life pleasing to our God and Savior, Jesus Christ.

This book is meant to be a guide for biblical counselors on how to effectively help counselees overcome their struggles, practical and spiritual, and become true, faithful disciples of Jesus. My approach to biblical counseling can be broken down into eight essential steps, each rooted in biblical disciple-making principles. I will clearly describe each step, how and where it is taught in Scripture, and why it is vital to strengthening discipleship.

Discipleship, or becoming a true follower of Jesus, comes from the example set by early believers as described in the book of Acts. They were labeled "Christians" because they reminded people of Jesus Christ and what He taught. In other words, they were true disciples who resembled their Master and reflected His teaching through their attitudes, values, actions, and treatment of others.

The goal of biblical counseling is to help people become a consistently positive influence in the church, giving rather than merely receiving. Contributing to the church in this way is a signal that the person has become a true disciple of Jesus Christ.

What is biblical counseling? Simply stated, it's helping people solve their problems. It's about discovering the cause, then applying biblical principles to help them overcome their problems, and giving them the necessary tools for them to move forward in their spiritual maturity.

That goal can be accomplished by studying and applying the following principles I shall refer to as the eight "I"s. These important steps are as follows:

- INVOLVEMENT: building warm, caring friendships and influential relationships
- INSPIRATION: inspiring people with biblical hope
- INVENTORY: collecting and considering data on the people who come to us: their background (education, parents, job, etc.), physical condition, strengths and weaknesses (both spiritual and in their character), key relationships, the pressures they face, etc.
- INTERPRETATION: using "inventory" gathered in relation to biblical teaching to interpret the nature and cause of a person's problems
- INSTRUCTION: giving biblical guidance on how to understand the conclusion made in the "interpretation" phase, and then setting goals to solve the problem(s)
- INDUCEMENT: using biblical teaching to inspire strong, godly principles in the person and to motivate him or her to reach the goals of "instruction"
- IMPLEMENTATION: discussing how to make specific changes in the person's life to reach the goals established during "inducement" through practical, biblically motivated steps
- INTEGRATION: checking in with the person and evaluating

his progress in reaching the set goals using the steps established in "implementation." This allows us to focus on preserving progress while addressing persistent issues.

Surely every writer wants his books to have an impact on people. What do I hope to accomplish with this book?

- Provide a biblical foundation for using the Scriptures in dealing with your own spiritual problems and the spiritual problems of others;
- Demonstrate the value of using the Bible, rather than worldly wisdom, to deal with problems;
- Familiarize the reader with the issues that people face and give an accurate paradigm for evaluating them so the necessary assistance can be provided;
- Enlarge compassion and the ability to help others make biblical changes and become better disciples of Jesus Christ;
- Provide a procedure to use in dealing with any counseling situation—in your own life as well as the lives of others;
- Challenge the personal and spiritual development necessary to qualify a believer to minister to others.

Before we get into the opening chapters, it is important to discuss some strategic, foundational issues. Every counseling system is based on certain presuppositions or on a certain belief system. These presuppositions dictate one's method or practice in counseling. They reflect a counselor's personal theological convictions.

Freud, for example, used the strategy of dream analysis, free association, hypnosis, and early childhood experience because of his personal doctrinal convictions about the nature of man and the causes of man's problems. Rogers used the strategy of UPR, and client-centered therapy, and focused on building self-esteem because of his convictions about the nature of man and the causes of man's problems. Skinner used the technique of behavior modification, positive reinforcement, and aversive therapy because of his convictions about the nature of man and the causes of man's problems.

Secular psychology starts on a flawed premise. It says that men are basically born good, but their genetic makeup, environment, and experiences shape them into the flawed, confused, sometimes criminal people they become. This is the exact opposite to the Christian doctrine of total depravity which says that every person is born a sinful, rebellious creature and that it is only by the grace of our merciful God that one can be changed.

Ultimately, all counselors are theologians, aren't they? Some are sound and some are not. If your foundational presuppositions are based upon anything other than the holy Word of God, then you will fall into the latter group. These misguided counselors may have their clients' best interests at heart, but they mislead them as they are themselves misled. Their views of truth and reality, the nature of man, and the causes of his problems are reflected in the methods they use to try to help people—and all are based on unbiblical convictions.

As Christians, we must make sure that the methods or strategies we use in our attempt to help people change are truly based upon Scripture and are in harmony with solid biblical theology. Our methodology ought to consistently reflect sound theology. Therefore, what we do and why we do it flows out of what we believe. What this means is that if we are to be truly biblical in our method, we must be very clear about our fundamental beliefs.

A brief overview of some major doctrines we must hold to

1. Biblical counseling is based upon a biblical understanding of the doctrine of God: *Theology*. These doctrinal truths about God have tremendous implications for us as we seek to counsel people.
    a. God is Triune (three Persons). 2 Corinthians 13:14; John 1:1–3; Romans 9:5; and is one God. Deuteronomy 6:4–5; 1 Timothy 2:5.
    b. God is Creator—Jeremiah 32:17; Genesis 1:1
    c. God is Holy—Isaiah 6:3; 1 Peter 1:16.
    d. God is loving, gracious and merciful—1 John 4:8; Ephesians 2:4; Galatians 2:20.

29

    e. God is unchangeable or immutable—Hebrews 13:8; James 1:17.

    f. God is all-knowing and all-wise; omniscient —Romans 11:33; Psalm 139; 1 John 3:20; Hebrews 4:13.

    g. God is omnipresent—Psalm 139; Matthew 28:20.

    h. God is truthful. He cannot lie—Hebrews 6:18; Titus 1:2; Isaiah 65:16; 1 John 5:20.

    i. God is faithful, trustworthy—1 Corinthians 10:13; 1:9; 2 Corinthians 1:18; 1 John 1:9.

2. Biblical counseling is based on a biblical perspective on the doctrine of knowledge: *Epistemology*—what is truth and how do we come to know it?

    a. Knowledge of truth is vitally important—John 8:32.

    b. We are sanctified by the truth—John 17:19.

    c. It is good and acceptable to God that we come to the knowledge of the truth—1 Timothy 2:3-4.

    d. The truth produces godliness—Titus 1:1.

    e. Whatever truth God reveals in His Word is authoritative—Psalm 119:128; Isaiah 8:19-20; 2 Timothy 3:16.

    f. This truth is sufficient to enable us to live godly lives pleasing to Christ—2 Peter 1:3-4; 2 Timothy 3:16-17; Psalm 19:7-11; Psalm 119.

        i. This means it is unnecessary to add anything to the Scriptures to live godly lives.

        ii. No other writings are of equal value to the Scriptures.

        iii. We should not consider any ideas of man from outside the Scriptures as being necessary for us to live and function as God wants us to.

        iv. We should not consider anything to be sin if it is not forbidden by Scripture either explicitly or by implication.

        v. We should not consider anything that is not clearly commanded by Scripture to be a requirement for godly living.

        vi. Our living and counseling should only emphasize what Scripture emphasizes.

vii. We should make full use of and depend upon the truths of Scripture rather than extrabiblical ideas, concepts, methodologies, and/or practices.

3. Biblical counseling is based upon a biblical perspective on the doctrine of man: *Anthropology*.
   a. Man is made in the image of God. Because of that, antibiblical methods are wrong. This includes biochemical determinism, secular environmental determinism, behaviorism, victim mentality, and humanistic psychology (the idea that man has all he needs within himself).
   b. Man is a worshiping being. He was made to worship and serve God. Therefore, his relationship with God is the most important factor in his life. Man was not made to be an autonomous being. He will and does worship either the true God or a false one.
   c. Man is directed by his heart, therefore any system of counseling that ignores the heart misses the heart of the issue. Behaviorism and legalism that focus primarily on actions and behavior are wrong.
   d. Man is a psychosomatic being made up of two important parts—the inner man and the outer man. No counseling system that ignores either of these aspects is biblical.

4. Biblical counseling is based on a biblical perspective on the doctrine of sin: *Hamartiology*.
   a. Sin has its corporate aspects.
   b. Sin is hereditary. Man is not born good or innocent. "In Adam's Fall, We Sinned All."[2]
   c. Sin has its habitual aspects. Slavery to sin is very real. We develop sinful manners of life (habits, patterns of thinking, responses, desires, lifestyle patterns). Sanctification is a process involving the need to put off and put on. It requires practice and training.
   d. Sin has its conscious, personal aspects. Willful acts do occur. Guilt is real and a sense of guilt can be beneficial. Sin is a personal disobedience or rebellion against God.

2 From the opening of the *New England Catechism*.

5. Biblical counseling is based on a biblical perspective on the doctrine of Christ and salvation: *Christology* and *Soteriology*.
   a. Christ is the God-man. Thus, He reveals God to us, is the mediator between God and man, and is the ultimate Prophet, Priest, and King.
   b. Christ is our perfect substitute. On our behalf He
      i. Kept the law perfectly for us;
      ii. Lived a sinless, perfect life for us;
      iii. Died a substitutionary death as the Lamb of God. He is the propitiation for our sins;
      iv. Is the model or example of what we should be.
   c. Christ is the ascended Lord who
      i. Sits at the Father's right hand in glory;
      ii. Conquered sin, sickness, demons, and death;
      iii. Sent the Holy Spirit who alone can change our hearts and give us victory;
      iv. Will come again in power and glory.

6. Biblical counseling is based on a biblical perspective on the doctrine of the Holy Spirit: *Pneumatology*.
   a. The Holy Spirit is a Person (the third Person of the Godhead). He is the ultimate Counselor, focuses on Christ and His activity, and always uses the Word of God.
   b. The Holy Spirit is necessary for a good counselor to do his job. Supernatural wisdom and power from the Holy Spirit is needed for a person to counsel effectively.
   c. The Holy Spirit is necessary for the counselee to change. He is the only means of genuine change. Behavior modification is a short-term fix, but change produced by the Holy Spirit is lasting and effective.

7. Biblical counseling is based on a biblical perspective on the doctrine of the church: *Ecclesiology*.
   a. The church is His body. Christ is the Head of the church, which is the temple of the Holy Spirit. The church, when teaching sound doctrine, is sufficient for evangelism, instruction, edification, and discipling. Other self-help groups are unnecessary.

b. The church and its leaders have been given authority by God. No state, government, or organization has been given this authority. It is the church's mandate to preach God's Word, to guide, counsel, and disciple the flock.

8. Biblical counseling is based on a biblical perspective on the doctrine of the end times: *Eschatology.*
   a. God is sovereign over history—now and forever.
   b. Christ is in control. He has defeated the world, the flesh, and the devil. Humble prayer and dependence upon Him are important aspects of counseling.
   c. Christ's present reign as King of kings gives hope for the present.
   d. Christ's second coming gives hope for the future.
   e. Christ's return should motivate us to greater holiness and perseverance.

These are the foundational presuppositions necessary for effective biblical counseling. They provide a starting point upon which we can build.

Counselees discover that real, substantial biblical change is possible in their lives. Their toughest interpersonal problems can be overcome. Christ provides that hope, and it is through Him and the empowering work of the Holy Spirit that we can reassure them that their struggles now have an end in sight.

Before we tackle the eight "I"s of biblical counseling, I think it prudent to define some important terms. Here are a few:

• SIN: Missing the mark of obedience to God's commands. Biblical terms for sin = rebellion, perversion, emptiness, lostness, foolishness, the world's worst tyrant, slavery. It covers any lack of conformity to God's Word (by omission or commission) in thought, desire, attitude, emotion, action, and/or reaction.
• REGENERATION: New life. This word indicates the moment a person is brought from spiritual death to spiritual life.
• JUSTIFICATION: A once-for-all forensic act of God wherein He declares a person righteous through the imputed righ-

teousness of Christ.

- SANCTIFICATION: the process of progressive spiritual maturity in which a person becomes transformed into greater and greater Christlikeness.
- REPENTANCE: An awareness of and turning away from sin.
- FAITH: Complete confidence and trust. It is "the assurance of things hoped for, the conviction of things not seen" (Hebrews 11:1).
- GRACE: Unmerited favor (**G**od's **R**edemption **A**t **C**hrist's **E**xpense).
- HOPE: A biblically based certainty and confident expectation that what God has promised will most certainly take place.
- LOVE: Rather than mere affection or feeling, love is more appropriately seen as a verb. It involves mind, will, and action. It is how one should treat others.
- DISCIPLINE: Exercising self-control, choosing to do the right thing and doing it because it is the right thing.
- OBEDIENCE: The external and internal positive response to what God has said.
- HEART: The mission control center of a person's life.
- DEHABITUATION/REHABITUATION: This involves the putting off of the old manner of life and putting on a new manner of life. This is practiced until it becomes a new habit or manner of life.
- CONFESSION: Awareness of sin compels a person to acknowledge it to God.
- COMMITMENT: Making a resolution to trust and obey, regardless of the consequences.
- GODLINESS: Devotion to God. This love, fear, and supreme devotion to God manifests itself in living a life that is pleasing to Him.
- GUILT: Culpability for breaking God's law.
- IDOLATRY: Giving anything or anyone the worship, obedience, attention, trust, and service that only God deserves.
- LEGALISM: Seeking to be saved (or sanctified) by one's own works. Finding one's security, assurance and satisfaction in what one does or has done rather than in the grace of God and in what Christ has done or is doing.

- LIFE-DOMINATING PROBLEMS: Sins that affect and negatively influence many aspects of a person's life.
- CHURCH DISCIPLINE: Bringing the authority of the church to bear on an unrepentant member. This may include encouragement, exhortation, confrontation, instruction, accountability, admonition, rebuke, reproof, and even disfellowshipment (being excluded from church membership).
- HOMEWORK: This includes reading assignments, journaling, Bible study projects, etc. Biblical counselors utilize and design these activities to challenge and teach, providing opportunities to dive into the Word, allowing the Holy Spirit to work in the counselee's heart and mind and bring about genuine change.
- FEELING ORIENTATION: When a person makes decisions about what is right or wrong on the basis of his or her own feelings instead of the Word of God. This person lives to please self rather than God.
- COMPLICATING PROBLEMS: Negative consequences that have developed as a result of another sin.
- NONVERBAL COMMUNICATION: Messages conveyed by behavior, expression, and/or body language. An effective biblical counselor is observant to this unspoken communication.
- PRESENTATION PROBLEM: The initial problem that brings someone to a counselor for help.
- RESPONSIBILITY: Being willing to focus on personal sins and failures without blaming others.
- HOLINESS: Internal and external conformity to God and His Word.
- LEARNED BEHAVIOR: Developing an unbiblical way of thinking or living by observing others.

This book excites me. My entire career has led me to this point of sharing these essential steps with others who desire to make a difference in the lives of hurting people. As I've already stated, this book is for parents wanting to disciple their children, for pastors wanting to disciple their flock, for counselors seeking to help others by using the sufficient Word of God, and for all believers who want to improve the quality of their own devotion and obedience to our Father.

Now, it is with great pleasure that I introduce you to the eight "I"s.

1

The 8 "I"s

Biblical counseling is inherently practical. If it's not practical, what possible good is it? The goal of biblical counseling is to help people, after all. It does this by putting the principles of Scripture into practice in their lives. Biblical change is possible in every area of life—in thoughts, desires, words, and actions.

In what has come to be known as The Great Commission, Christ told His disciples, "All authority in heaven and on earth has been given to me. *Go therefore and make disciples of all nations, baptizing them in the name of the Father and of the Son and of the Holy Spirit, teaching them to observe all that I have commanded you.* And behold, I am with you always, to the end of the age" (Matthew 28:18–20, emphasis added).

That's what biblical counseling accomplishes. It enables the people of God to

- Make disciples of all nations;
- Baptize them in the name of the Father and of the Son and of the Holy Spirit;
- Teach them to observe all the commands of Christ.

We cannot counsel people biblically if they are not believers in Christ. Unbelievers do not acknowledge the authority of Christ or the Bible, and are under no compunction to follow the principles taught by Scripture. In fact, we are told in 1 Corinthians 2:14,

"The natural person does not accept the things of the Spirit of God, for they are folly to him, and he is not able to understand them because they are spiritually discerned."

So, the first task of the biblical counselor is to ascertain the spiritual standing of the one who comes for help. Is he a believer in the Lord Jesus Christ? Is that person prepared to come under His authority and, thus, the authority of Scripture?

If that person has, in fact, come to know Jesus as Lord and Savior, the counselor can move on. If not, evangelism must be the first item on the agenda. Without the power of the indwelling Holy Spirit, true biblical change is impossible. Without it, all that can be accomplished is some semblance of behavior modification, which likely will fade as soon as the counselee's immediate problem is resolved.

Therefore, biblical counseling is evangelistic.

Next, there is the responsibility to baptize. This is a natural step in the lives of new believers who desire to obey God. Biblical counselors encourage these new believers to take this step in their local church. We can help facilitate this important step.

Next, we are to teach the person to follow all that Christ has commanded in His Word. This is where the strongest emphasis of the eight "I"s is devoted. It is in this area that most of my comments will be directed. We must teach our counselees the principles involved, making sure they understand the biblical commands. Then we must help them implement these changes in their own lives. What a remarkable, heavy, gratifying privilege we have to be a part of this plan.

By learning and understanding the commands of Christ, our counselees are enabled to apply these truths through the grace of God and the power of the Holy Spirit. These truths become tools they can use for the rest of their lives.

That's why biblical counseling is so practical. It changes people's lives.

Two ways to use the model
I'm presenting through the eight "I"s

This biblical model of counseling can be used in two ways—as a *guideline* and as a *checklist*. Used as a guideline, it provides specific direction as we attempt to help people in the process of change. Used as a checklist, it evaluates the worthiness or success of our attempts to help people change.

Guideline: Many passages tell us what we are to do in counseling others—like Matthew 28:19-20, Colossians 1:28, Colossians 3:16, 1 Thessalonians 5:11, 14, Galatians 6:1, to name a few. Some even give general directions about how to do it—by teaching, preaching and counseling. However, they don't really give specific directions in helping people change.

As a result, many people want to help but don't know how. They sometimes feel inadequate and don't know where to start. The desire is there, but the know-how is not. Because of this, counselors need guidelines if they are to increase in effectiveness. That's what this book provides—a model for *how* to do this important work in the lives of others.

Checklist: A checklist evaluates the success of our attempts to help people overcome their struggles with biblical change. Without a checklist, how can we determine if we're doing the right thing? What criteria do we use to determine the worth of our efforts in discipling?

First, let's discuss a *wrong* way to determine our effectiveness. Some think of successful counseling in terms of immediate, visible results, which can be misleading. The fruit of the Spirit is difficult to quantify. (See Mark 10:17-21, Mark 4:26-28, 2 Tim. 4:10, Rev. 3:17-21, or Matt. 7:21-23, for example.)

So, what are some of the right ways to measure our effectiveness? The first is this: Have I done what the Lord wants me to do in my discipling efforts? Have I been true to the Word of God? (See 2 Tim. 2:24-25, 1 Cor. 4:1-2, Luke 12:42, Matt. 25:14-23, 2 Cor. 5:9, for example.)

We face two real dangers in our attempts to help people change. One is the danger of taking our responsibility too lightly—being flippant, sloppy, and/or unprepared.

The other is being excessively concerned with our own responsibility and beginning to perceive that the result of our counseling depends on *us*! If the one we're counseling doesn't have a good result, we feel the weight of guilt, that we must not have said enough or done enough. We feel that it must be our fault. We end up discouraged and afraid to try again.

Therefore, understanding and utilizing these eight key elements as a guideline and as a checklist can keep us from both of these dangers. They keep us from being flippant because they remind us that God uses means to accomplish His work. He's the One who blesses and uses His faithful servants for good in the lives of His people.

These elements help us to remember what being faithful involves. They keep us from depending too much on visible results as our criteria for measuring our effectiveness. If we can honestly say that we've done these things and still don't see any change, then we still must say we were effective in our efforts.

Success or failure doesn't depend on us. If we've been faithful, we don't have to be discouraged or afraid to try again because we've done what is pleasing to the Lord. What He wants from us is faithfulness.

Overview of the eight key elements of promoting biblical change—the eight "I"s

The biblical process of making disciples and accomplishing biblical change involves two primary aspects—putting off bad fruit and putting on good fruit. This concept is familiar to any student of the Bible.

One such familiar passage is in Ephesians 4:20–24: "But that is not the way you learned Christ!—assuming that you have heard about him and were taught in him, as the truth is in Jesus, *to put off your old self*, which belongs to your former manner of life and is corrupt through deceitful desires, and to be renewed in the spirit of your minds, and *to put on the new self*, created after the likeness of God in true righteousness and holiness" (emphasis added).

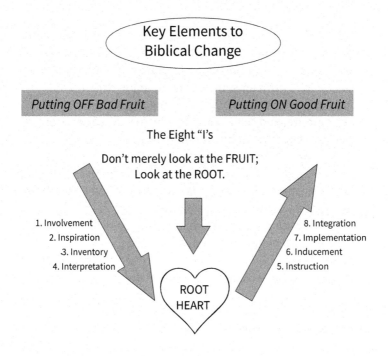

Note that the first four "I"s focus primarily, though not exclusively, on the "putting off" aspect of biblical change. The last four focus mainly on the "putting on" aspect of biblical change.

Definitions of these eight key elements of biblical change

- *Involvement*: Promotes biblical change by establishing a change-facilitating relationship.
- *Inspiration:* According to Webster's dictionary, inspiration involves influencing, stimulating, arousing or producing a thought or feeling. In this case, in promoting biblical change, we want to inspire, arouse or influence the counsel-ee to develop and sustain an attitude and feeling of hope that will promote biblical change.
- *Inventory/Investigation:* Promotes biblical change by secur-

ing enough of the right kinds of information to accurately understand the counselee and his problems.

- *Interpretation:* Promotes biblical change by analyzing and organizing the information we have gathered so we can accurately identify the biblical nature and cause(s) of the counselee's problems, then convincingly explain them.

- *Instruction:* Promotes biblical change by giving accurate, appropriate, and relevant biblical instruction that provides God's perspective on how to solve the problem(s).

- *Inducement:* Promotes biblical change by encouraging (inducing, persuading) the counselee to repent of sinful attitudes, words, and actions, and make a decisive commitment to obey the Lord and follow biblical directives.

- *Implementation:* Promotes biblical change by helping the counselee to plan how to make the biblical directives a reality in his life.

- *Integration:* Promotes biblical change by coaching and mentoring the counselee until the necessary changes are integrated into his or her life, encouraging integration into the life of the church.

In this book, we'll discuss each of these elements individually. In practice, however, you will find they can't be as neatly separated. In the counseling setting, it's much more common to engage in several of them at the same time.

2

Involvement

The first "I" is Involvement. We said in the last chapter that involvement promotes biblical change by establishing a change-facilitating relationship. How does it do that? What is a change-facilitating relationship?

This chapter will flesh that out. Several purposes in discussing this key element are:

- Demonstrating the importance of involvement in the counseling process;
- Defining what involvement is;
- Describing biblical ways of building this necessary involvement into your counseling relationships.

To do this, let's examine a particular case study utilizing involvement.

> Her name was Clara. A member of a local church, Clara came to her pastor in tears, explaining to him that her marriage had become so oppressive that she could no longer remain with her husband. She had made the decision to file for divorce on the grounds of mental and bodily cruelty.
>
> Her pastor asked her to reconsider this course of action until they could meet to talk about this further. Clara had no hope that anything could change her marriage—or her mind—but she agreed to meet with him.

During the first session, the pastor gathered data and tried to encourage her with some information and promises from God's Word. He told her that before she proceeded with the divorce, she ought to try to work out the problems between her and her husband through biblical counseling. He then asked her to postpone divorce proceedings until they had time to do some biblical counseling. Clara reluctantly agreed.

At the end of the session, he set a time to meet with Clara again. He gave her some homework assignments which she committed to do before their next session. The homework was to read Chapter 7 of a book called *God's Solutions to Life's Problems* and complete the questions included in the chapter. He also asked her to read *Christ and Your Problems* and write down five important lessons that applied to her in her personal situation, and he instructed her to ask her husband to come with her to the next counseling session.

When she returned for the second session, it was obvious that she was extremely angry and upset. She began by saying with a snarl, "You asked me to bring my husband with me. Well, I tried to get him here, but he had other things to do. I can only imagine what those are! See? He's such a jerk. He couldn't care less about our marriage."

The pastor responded. "Clara, I don't want to hear such charges behind Marty's back. You said before that you told him you forgave him. It's apparent that you are continuing to be hostile toward him in spite of that fact. It seems to me that you have made little or no attempt to bury the issues and start afresh. I'm beginning to think you don't truly understand forgiveness."

Clara blurted, "What? Forgive him? You want me to forgive him? You want me to bury what he's done to me over so many years? Pastor, there's a limit to what a woman can endure. Oh, I could forgive him for the times he's hit me and said mean things to me. I could forgive him for the times he has wasted our money on frivolous things. What I can't forgive is discovering him in *our* bed with that other woman. How can you *possibly* ask me to forgive that? Ugh. He's just an immature, immoral, animalistic pig who doesn't deserve forgiveness. Doesn't God oppose such behavior in His Word? He deserves nothing but punishment for what he's put me through."

The pastor said, "Clara, again, let me caution you about making such charges against him. I want to help you, but I'm not here to salve your bruised ego and listen to your complaints about Marty."

Clara's eyes filled with tears. Sobbing, she said, "You just don't understand. Didn't you hear me? *I'm* not the one who has committed adultery. I was willing to come for counseling. Marty isn't. I'm the one who joined the church. Marty didn't. So why are you siding with him against me?"

Let's pull up here to answer some questions about this case study and what has happened thus far. I encourage you to think through these questions and answer them yourself.

1. What has Clara said about what has happened in her marriage?
2. What tendencies might a counselor show in responding to people like Clara?
3. How would you characterize the counselor's response or approach to Clara?
4. What does he seem to think her main problem or greatest need is at this point?
5. Do you agree with the counselor's assessment of her greatest need and problem at this moment?
6. What impact did his response have on Clara?
7. What might he have done differently that might have defused rather than exacerbated the situation?

Though his intention was to help, the pastor seems to have forgotten or lost sight of a few important facts regarding his counselee. First of all, if he is to be an *effective* counselor, he must keep in mind that Clara is a person who has been grievously sinned against. She's hurt, angry, and bitter—and with good reason. Clara feels misused, mistreated, rejected, hopeless, and betrayed.

Because of her husband's behavior, she feels justified in what she is thinking about doing. Also, because of her experience with Marty, she is likely sensitive to anything that resembles rejection or condemnation. Filled with such self-pity and pain, she is not ready to be admonished and rebuked.

Counseling requires much thought, insight, and prayer. The counselor must find a way to minister to Clara's needs without coming across as uncaring and clueless about her pain. Some people develop a *problem-centered* approach to counseling. Once they discover the problem, they want to quickly deal with it, expecting the counselee to take their sage advice and run with it. Problem solved.

It's not as simple as that. Effective biblical counselors take a *people-centered* approach. It's more about the person than about the problem.

In this case, the pastor has opted for taking a confrontive, behavioristic approach. He seems to think her biggest problem is her failure to forgive. I think her greatest problem is that she has lost the sense of God's presence with her. Her relationship with Him at this point is shallow. She likely feels abandoned and betrayed by God as well as by her husband and other people.

At this point she is not capable of receiving this kind of stern counsel. By approaching her in this way, the pastor is violating the principle found in John 16:12. In this passage, Jesus recognizes His disciples' inability to process more than they can accept. "I still have many things to say to you, but you cannot bear them now." (This same compassion toward deeply hurt people can also be seen in John 4 and John 8.)

To me, Clara needs two things in order to handle her situation in a godly fashion. First of all, she must be helped to develop a deeper and closer relationship with Christ. Only then will she have the strength to properly handle the awful situation she's in. Next, and of secondary importance, Clara needs to develop that closer relationship through the counsel of a godly person she views as a friend, not a foe—an ally and not an adversary.

Read 1 Thessalonians 2:1, 13. The results of this teaching are noted in 1:9–10. Why did Paul's teaching have such an impact? The ultimate reason is found in 2:13. "And we also thank God constantly for this, that when you received the word of God, which you heard from us, you accepted it not as the word of men but as what it really is, the word of God, which is at work in you believers." The Thessalonians listened to Paul, were impacted by his message, and were brought into a deep relationship with God through a caring relationship with Paul. (See also 1 Thess. 2:7–9, Acts 20:36–37, Acts 21:13.)

This is true of any good, effective counseling relationship. We must keep in mind the truths of Proverbs 27:6, 9. "Faithful are the wounds of a friend; profuse are the kisses of an enemy. . . . Oil and perfume make the heart glad, and the sweetness of a friend comes from his earnest counsel."

In light of this, and many other verses, an effective biblical counselor builds involvement through compassion, respect, and sincerity. People need to see these qualities in the one they've turned to for help.

When someone is sinned against, he commonly feels pain, hurt, fear, and hardship. As effective counselors, we must try to promote biblical actions rather than sinful reactions. And we do that through involvement in their lives and their thinking.

Sinned Against

Prevent   Pain, Hurt, Fear   Promote
                 Hardship, etc.

Sinful Reaction: Biblical Action:

Evil for Evil, Malice   Good for Evil,
Retaliation, Evil Speaking   Prayer,
Promiscuity, Drugs, Suicide   Trust, Self Control
Defensiveness, Distrust   Solution-Oriented
Hostility, etc.   Actions, etc.

Too many times, offering advice without first developing a caring relationship means that advice will fall upon deaf ears. Hurting people may not care what you have to say if they do not see genuine compassion and involvement.

As I mentioned in the previous chapter, it is impossible for an unbeliever to experience true biblical change. The following is also true. An application of biblical principles without developing a deeper relationship with God produces no change or only a change that is pharisaical or legalistic. It results in nothing more than behavior modification.

True compassion desires to see a closer relationship to the Lord as a result of counseling. Only then will the counselee have the tools available to sustain him through all the trials and tribulations of life. Such a counselee leaves the counseling setting prepared for any situation.

It rarely starts out that way, though. When a hurting person first comes to a counselor, all he can see is his painful circumstance or situation. God's involvement in that is far outside his thinking, in most cases.

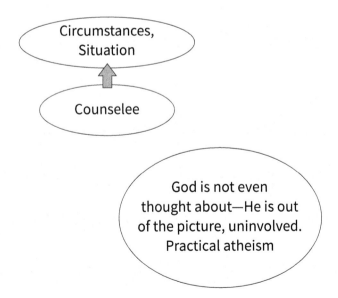

In Stage 2 of counseling, the hurting person is beginning to see through his circumstances to embrace the promises, truths, and lovingkindness of God. He begins to see his life through the lens of Scripture. He experiences a greater closeness to the Father as He draws such a person to Himself through the suffering.

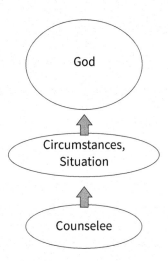

In Stage 3, the final stage, we see a change in the counselee's perspective of his problems, of God's involvement, in the Holy Spirit's empowerment, and in his appreciation of the Bible and the principles contained in it. The counselor takes a back seat to this greater awareness as the counselee embraces the truths and promises of Scripture and is able to apply it to life. It's a beautiful change in mindset brought about through effective counseling. This is why true biblical counseling is inherently practical. It changes lives!

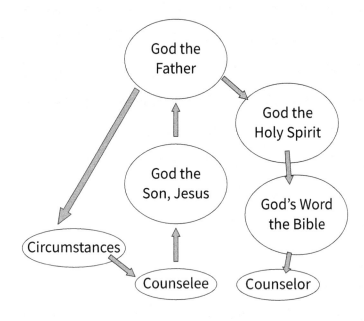

What is involved in building this deep involvement that facilitates biblical change? What disposes people to listen to us and receive the counsel we bring? As I search the Scriptures, I see several factors in building this change-facilitating relationship with people.

The first one is compassion. It plays a vital role in the effectiveness of discipleship. "Put on then, as God's chosen ones, holy and beloved, compassion, kindness, humility, meekness, and patience" (Col. 3:12). (Also see Eph. 4:32, Phil. 2:1–2, and 1 Peter 3:8.)

The Bible gives us clear examples to follow in dealing gently with one another. We have the examples of history's two greatest counselors—Jesus and Paul.

Jesus, called by Isaiah "Wonderful Counselor" (Isa. 9:6), is the greatest example. We can't read the Bible without being impressed with the fact that His life was characterized by compassion. I'll mention a few passages here, but there are many, many more I could have chosen.

- Matthew 9:36—"When he saw the crowds, he had compassion for them . . ."
- Matthew 14:14—"When he went ashore he saw a great crowd, and he had compassion on them and healed their sick."
- Matthew 15:32—"Then Jesus called his disciples to him and said, 'I have compassion on the crowd . . .'"
- Luke 7:13—"And when the Lord saw her, he had compassion on her and said to her, 'Do not weep.'"
- Hebrews 4:15—"For we do not have a high priest who is unable to sympathize with our weaknesses, but one who in every respect has been tempted as we are, yet without sin."

The apostle Paul was also a great counselor, full of compassion. Here are a few verses, out of many I could have chosen, which point to his great compassion—which was key to his effective ministry.

- Acts 20:31—"Therefore be alert, remembering that for three years I did not cease night or day to admonish everyone with tears."
- Acts 20:19—". . .serving the Lord with all humility and with tears . . ."
- Philippians 1:7— "It is right for me to feel this way about you all, because I hold you in my heart, for you are all partakers with me of grace . . ."
- Galatians 4:19— ". . .my little children, for whom I am again in the anguish of childbirth until Christ is formed in you!"
- Romans 9:1-3— "I am speaking the truth in Christ—I am not lying; my conscience bears me witness in the Holy Spirit—that I have great sorrow and unceasing anguish in my heart. For I could wish that I myself were accursed and cut off from Christ for the sake of my brothers . . . ."

How can we cultivate or develop genuine compassion? Do we automatically have it when we come to Christ as our Savior? Is there anything we can do to increase in compassion and godly kindness? And if we do have genuine compassion, how is it manifested in the way we treat others?

We're given some godly suggestions from the Bible in how we are to increase in this area. For one thing, we can study the life of Christ and highlight passages describing His compassion toward His people. Then we can pray that the Holy Spirit would empower us to follow His example in our own dealings with others.

Another means of acquiring deeper compassion in the way we treat others is to remind ourselves of our own need. Because of Christ's great mercy to us, we are now in the family of God. He loved us while we were unlovable. He gave His very life for us. His compassion for His people is demonstrated in His work of grace in salvation. How can we not show compassion for others, after receiving such compassion from our Lord?

Another way to experience compassion is putting ourselves in their shoes. Think about what this hurting person is going through and try to figure out how he must feel, what he must be thinking, and how helpless and hopeless he feels about finding a solution to his pain.

We must learn to see life through the eyes of those we long to disciple. What does life look like from their perspective? Listen to them. We must take time to sit where they sit before rushing in with our "sage advice." We must employ compassion before we open our mouths.

It is often helpful to associate yourself with other compassionate people. Spend time with hard-hearted friends who do not demonstrate godly compassion for others and you'll find their attitudes creeping into your own thinking. Spend time with compassionate people and pray their godly influence impacts you in a deep way.

Another way to improve our compassion for others is to view them as brethren, as part of our family. These people, believers in our Lord Jesus Christ, are not strangers. They are members of our own family. We are coheirs with them in the promises of heaven. Don't we go the extra mile to help our natural family members? Why shouldn't we then go that extra mile for those in our spiritual one?

Remember James 4:2b. "You do not have, because you do not ask." Perhaps the best way to improve this area of compassion is to ask for it! Make it a priority in your life to ask the Holy Spirit to give you this increase. Prayer is the most effective way to influence godly compassion.

How is genuine compassion manifested in the life of a Christian? Here are a few ways, using a few of many verses I could have chosen:

- Through words (1 Thess. 2:12–13)
- Through prayer (Phil. 1:9, Eph. 1:15–16)
- Through genuine grief in connection with their pain (Mark 3:1–5, John 11:32–35)
- Through gentleness and tenderness (Matt. 12:20, 1 Thess. 5:14)
- Through concern for physical and spiritual needs and doing what you can to meet those needs (Mark 8:1–3)

Compassion is shown in so many other ways, like offering encouragement, by not pushing people too fast, by speaking in a gracious manner, by maintaining self-control in the face of insults, by defending people who are being mistreated or falsely accused, and by sacrificing time and money to help others. One thing is certain—a hurting person recognizes compassion when it can be seen in whatever form it takes.

What kinds of things demonstrate a lack of compassion? Even compassionate people may be guilty of some of these things without being aware. Don't assume your innocence. Review this list and see if there are ways you can improve your counselees' perception of your level of compassion.

What not to do:

- Smirking at them, at their stories;
- Interrupting them when they are talking;
- Yawning;
- Using Bible verses as a hammer or club over their heads;
- Accusing them of impure motives—especially without proof;
- Speaking to them in a scoffing, demeaning or disrespectful manner;
- Acting disinterested while they're talking (please don't

repeatedly look at your phone or watch in the middle of a counseling session);
* Making a joke out of their concerns.

Therefore, involvement is demonstrated through showing respect and compassion for the ones you seek to disciple. That includes a counselee, your children, or your brothers and sisters in Christ.

What nonverbal ways communicate interest in a counselor, friend or parent? I suggest an acronym I call SOLVER.

S—Squared shoulders
O—Open stance
L—Leaning slightly forward
V—Vocal quality
E—Eye contact
R—Relaxed posture

Other principles involved in demonstrating interest and attention can be shown by taking the other person's problem(s) seriously, by being appropriately warm and friendly, by refusing to be domineering or manipulative, by giving the person the benefit of the doubt (unless the facts prove to the contrary), and by commending the person's strengths, efforts, virtues, and successes.

As effective counselors, we must pattern what we're teaching. Therefore, we must hear the occasional disagreement and/or rebuke from that person without becoming defensive or intimidated. We must not respond in kind, but let love guide our responses. We must also guard the other person's reputation. We earn that person's trust when we do this and by keeping confidences. We demonstrate respect for him when we refuse to gossip about him or discuss his personal problems elsewhere.

Involvement is established through genuineness and honesty

These two traits, genuineness and honesty, should characterize the whole of our lives. However, in a counseling setting, they are imperative.

A primary verse that exemplifies this statement is 2 Corinthians 4:2. "But we have renounced disgraceful, under-handed ways. We refuse to practice cunning or to tamper with God's word, but by the open statement of the truth we would commend ourselves to everyone's conscience in the sight of God."

As a counselor, be honest about your credentials and qualifications, who and what you are. Don't pretend to be something you're not. Be honest about the kind of counseling you offer, and about what you expect of your counselee. Let him know what he can expect of you. (See 1 Corinthians 4:1.)

If in the course of counseling you misunderstand, make a mistake, are confused, or make a misstatement, be honest about those things as well. Admit them. Ask the counselee to forgive you. That goes for your children, too. Admitting your mistakes will cause them to think *more* highly of you, not less.

Involvement is promoted through the presence of the fruit of the spirit in the life of the counselor

Remember Galatians 5:22–23. "But the fruit of the Spirit is love, joy, peace, patience, kindness, goodness, faithfulness, gentleness, self-control; against such things there is no law."

Effective counselors must demonstrate these traits in life. No, they won't be able to lay claim on all of them to the same degree, and some they may still struggle with. Such is the work of the Holy Spirit in each of us. So, I'm not saying we show each of these traits perfectly. But I do think a counselor should be a mature believer, steadfast in faith, and sure-footed in theology. These are qualities that may be absent in those who seek our counsel. We can't encourage them in other people if we don't have them ourselves.

The fruit of the Spirit outlines qualities God desires for every Christian. Because of our standing in Him, developing these qualities is possible. The fact that they're called "fruit" indicates that they grow gradually—they ripen at different rates for each of us. Like fruit, these qualities require care and cultivation. These important qualities facilitate the development of good relationships. Let's look at each of these qualities a little more closely.

LOVE—Is love an emotion, a fond feeling? As I've said many times, I believe love is understood better as a verb than a noun. Love is how we treat one another. It is demonstrated by action, not only given lip service. Colossians 3:12–14 states: "Put on then, as God's chosen ones, holy and beloved, compassion, kindness, humility, meekness, and patience, bearing with one another and, if one has a complaint against another, forgiving each other; as the Lord has forgiven you, so you also must forgive. And above all these put on love, which binds everything together in perfect harmony." We must demonstrate love, compassion, and caring for those we disciple—and for one another. (See also 1 Corinthians 13 and remind yourself what Paul says about love there.)

JOY—A joyful person is a hopeful person. He is nice to be around, confident, with a positive outlook. A joyful person is easy to like and respect. Joy comes from within and is not dependent upon having a "happy" life. "For the kingdom of God is not a matter of eating and drinking but of righteousness and peace and joy in the Holy Spirit" (Rom. 14:17). Those we seek to influence for Christ must see joy in our hearts. (See also Phil. 4:11–13)

PEACE—We must have peace with God, the peace of God, and peace with one another. "Therefore, since we have been justified by faith, we have peace with God through our Lord Jesus Christ" (Rom. 5:1). We must not be pugnacious, contentious or critical in our relationships. Those we disciple must be able to follow our peaceful example. (See also Phil. 4:4–7)

PATIENCE—Oh, what a stumbling block for many believers! Yet, by the grace of God, we must cultivate this important quality in our own lives—for the benefit of others (and our own benefit) as well as to live a life pleasing to our Lord. "And we urge you, brothers, admonish the idle, encourage the fainthearted, help the weak, be patient with them all" (1 Thess. 5:14). A patient person will not be provoked or annoyed easily. He will be willing to calmly wait. He will not jump to conclusions, and will never become pushy or overbearing. Such a person is willing to hang in there, and to persevere. He doesn't give up quickly. Those we counsel may not "get it" as quickly as we hoped, but we must understand that people grow at different rates. We must be patient with their particular rate of progress. (See also Prov. 15:18)

KINDNESS—Much like compassion, this quality wants the best for others. Ephesians 4:32 states: "Be kind to one another, tender-hearted, forgiving one another, as God in Christ forgave you." We need to treat our counselees with kindness. They need to see it in the way we speak, the tone of our voice, and the affection with which we frame the instruction we offer. (See also Gen. 50:15–21 to remind yourself of Joseph's example of kindness to his brothers.)

GOODNESS—Similar to kindness, goodness is more about action. It seeks to promote the well-being of others. Goodness is often contrasted with evil. For example, "Do not be overcome by evil, but overcome evil with good" (Rom. 12:21). Some biblical examples of goodness to others are seen in the actions of the Good Samaritan, of the prodigal son's father, and of Barnabas. The effective counselor exemplifies goodness toward his counselees. (See also Gal. 6:10.)

FAITHFULNESS—Most often this is thought of as dependable, loyal, trustworthy, and reliable. We do what we say we will do. We practice what we preach. In season and out, we are consistently God-centered. "You then, my child, be strengthened by the grace that is in Christ Jesus, and what you have heard from me in the presence of many witnesses entrust to faithful men who will be able to teach others also" (2 Tim. 2:2). Our counselees must trust in our faithfulness to God—and to them. (See also Prov. 12:22.)

GENTLENESS—Often partnered with humility, gentleness is like a mother with her baby, like a gentle breeze, like soothing ointment. Gentleness refreshes and expresses a sense of love and kindness. It is not harsh or hurtful. It promotes calmness. Galatians 6:1 states: "Brothers, if anyone is caught in any transgression, you who are spiritual should restore him in a spirit of gentleness." The ones who come to us should fully rest in the fact that they are in a safe place, with a safe person, and obtaining safe, sound, biblical instruction. They come to us vulnerable and fearful. It's our job to make sure that's only a temporary initial condition and soon they will be able to rest in our presence. (See also 1 Thess. 2:7.)

SELF-CONTROL—This quality also seems elusive to us at times. Like patience, it's one that takes maturity to obtain. In one sense, it applies to physical sins of the flesh—of bodily appetites, thoughts, desires, lusts, words, actions, emotions, uses of time, money, and talents. We think of self-control as a physical attribute that keeps us out of trouble and in God's will. Paul writes thus in 1 Corinthians 9:27: "But I discipline my body and keep it under control, lest after preaching to others I myself should be disqualified."

There is another element, though, in self-control. This one concerns what goes on inwardly—our thought life, our attitudes, and the outflow of our hearts. The ones in our charge must know what to expect of us—that we will remain calm, composed, attentive, and not bristle if provoked. Let us serve as an example to them. (See also 2 Cor. 10:5.)

Summary of practical ways to demonstrate compassion and respect for the counselee

We've covered a lot of material in this chapter. I wanted to provide another list for you as a summary of the "rules of engagement" with a counselee. These rules are beneficial for every relationship in your life, so they will serve you well if you carry them out with others.

1. Remain alert and attentive.
2. Practice active listening. Don't allow your mind to wander.
3. Express interest with your face, eyes, and body posture.
4. Smile appropriately.
5. Weep appropriately.
6. Be on time. Don't make your counselee wait.
7. Be sensitive to your counselee's time frame.
8. Cancel appointments only when absolutely necessary.
9. Display gentleness when opposed.
10. Let your counselee talk before you share.

11. Don't give up on your counselee quickly.
12. Express appropriate optimism and a positive attitude about God's ability to help your counselee.
13. Speak in a warm, gentle tone of voice.
14. Express appreciation for your counselee's strengths, insights, efforts, changes, and any evidence of God's working in his life.
15. Take your counselee's problems seriously—never make light of his concerns.
16. Be available to your counselee. Send an encouraging note. Give your counselee a call when you think he is experiencing difficult times.
17. Offer your support in a non-judgmental manner.
18. Pray for your counselee within your sessions and assure him of your prayers during the week.
19. Encourage your counselee to call you if he is having an especially difficult time.

Involvement is established through fulfilling the next seven "I"s in the counseling process

Before moving on to the next chapter, I'd like to close with some thoughts about how involvement is going to affect each of the other keys to biblical change. I think you'll find that involvement is integral to each of the next seven "I"s in the series.

For one thing, involvement is developed through *inspiration*. It happens as you encourage a biblically based attitude of hope in the mind of your counselee.

It is developed as you take a thorough *inventory* and secure enough information to accurately understand the counselee and his problems.

Involvement is developed as you make an accurate *interpretation* of what your counselee is saying. It promotes biblical change by allowing you to analyze and organize that information so you can accurately and biblically identify the biblical nature and causes of the problem(s).

Involvement is encouraged as you promote biblical change by giving accurate, appropriate, and relevant biblical *instruction* that provides God's perspective on what to do to solve your counselee's problems.

It is developed as you *induce* (motivate, persuade) your counselee to repent of sinful attitudes, words, and actions, and to make a decisive commitment to obey the Lord and follow biblical directives.

Involvement is developed as you help your counselee to actually *integrate* the biblical directives and perspectives into the whole of his life.

So you see, involvement is "involved" in every aspect of counseling.

3

Inspiration

The second "I" is Inspiration. What do I mean by that? The Webster's definition is "influencing, stimulating, arousing or producing a thought or feeling." In the arena of biblical counseling, we desire to produce an attitude or feeling of *hope*.

In this chapter, my goals are to

1. Demonstrate the importance of promoting a solid attitude of biblical hope throughout the process of biblical change;
2. Present the characteristic features of true biblical hope;
3. Offer suggestions about godly ways to inspire the counselee to biblical hope.

In the last chapter, I provided a case study involving a woman I'm calling Clara. Her husband had committed adultery, treated her cruelly, and consistently rejected her.

We noted that Clara was angry, filled with self-pity, fear, discouragement, and despair. Yet, there is something else about Clara that we must not overlook. She clearly lacks hope! All her responses are symptomatic of her hopelessness. This is common with people experiencing anger and/or self-pity.

If a counselor is going to be able to effectively help her, he must not only establish involvement, but must also inspire her to have biblical hope. The truth is that Clara (and others like her) will not change—they will not respond to the difficult trials of life in a biblical way—unless they can be inspired to have an attitude of hopefulness. *Hope motivates change.*

This chapter will help you learn how to inspire that kind of hope—the kind that motivates change—into the lives of those you wish to help. The reason we'll focus so intently on this is not because this is the most important "I," but because they are all so intertwined, and inspiration is vital to the success of all the rest.

A person with strong hope will also have a lively faith and be a loving person. A person who lacks hope will also lack faith and love. He only seems to be able to look inside at his own pain and grief. Depression and self-pity do that—they turn people inward, causing them to withdraw and, yes, lose hope.

The Bible is filled with verses and passages that declare the importance of hope and describe what hope is and can do. Here are a few of many such passages:

- Hebrews 6:19-20—an anchor that keeps the soul
- 1 Thessalonians 4:13—keeps us from inordinate and excessive sorrow
- Proverbs 10:28—produces gladness
- Romans 5:2—helps us handle trials in a productive way
- Galatians 5:5—produces patience
- Hebrews 11:24-26—produces obedience
- 1 John 3:2—produces holiness, an aversion to sin
- 1 Thessalonians 1:3—produces perseverance and steadfastness
- Romans 15:4—produces peace
- Romans 12:12—produces joy
- Lamentations 3:18—produces physical and spiritual strength

Conversely, we can learn from these passages something about what happens when a person lacks hope. For instance, we deduce that a person lacks hope if he is

- Unstable
- Unmotivated
- Unhappy and discouraged; filled with self-pity; insecure
- Fearful
- Impatient

- Resistant to change
- Wishy-washy, easily swayed, tossed to and fro
- Despondent and despairing
- A blame shifter—highly critical; angry
- Disobedient
- Selfish
- Living in sin
- Spiritually weak
- A quitter, giving up on activities, people, and principles he once valued

I hope this list helps identify people who may be experiencing a lack of biblical hope in their lives. You will run across them. What can we do to help them find biblical hope again?

What is the essence of true biblical hope?

The way I define it is that it is an expectation of good based upon the promises of a God who cannot lie, on the promises of a God who will always do what He says He will do, a God who is absolutely trustworthy, a God who can always be relied upon, a God who will never go back on His Word. That is the God we serve.

Titus 1:2 states ". . . in hope of eternal life, which God, who never lies, promised before the ages began. . . ."

Then in 2 Peter 1:3–8, Peter makes some astounding statements. "His divine power has granted to us *all things that pertain to life and godliness,* through the knowledge of him who called us *to his own glory and excellence, by which he has granted to us his precious and very great promises,* so that through them you may become partakers of the divine nature, *having escaped from the corruption that is in the world* because of sinful desire. For this very reason, make every effort to supplement your faith with virtue, and virtue with knowledge, and knowledge with self-control, and self-control with steadfastness, and steadfastness with godliness, and godliness with brotherly affection, and brotherly affection with love. For *if these qualities are yours and are increasing, they keep you from being ineffective or unfruitful in the knowledge of our Lord Jesus Christ"* (emphasis added).

What an outstanding passage! "Everything we need for life and godliness." That's quite a promise.

The point of all of this is that we can do everything this passage describes by believing the promises our most glorious, excellent, powerful, never-lying God has made to us through Peter. He has given us everything we need to do all this.

Numbers 23:19 also contains wonderful truths about God that help alleviate despair and inspire us to be hopeful. It says, "God is not man, that he should lie, or a son of man, that he should change his mind. Has he said, and will he not do it? Or has he spoken, and will he not fulfill it?" This is a God we can hope in, trust, and believe. We can count on Him to do what He promises.

How about this one? "For all the promises of God find their Yes in him. That is why it is through him that we utter our Amen to God for his glory" (2 Cor. 1:20). This verse also provides a solid basis for being hopeful by reminding us that God keeps His promises.

Psalm 33:9 says, "For he spoke, and it came to be; he commanded, and it stood firm." God spoke and it was done. He spoke the universe into existence. This is power!

The last reference to mention is Romans 4:13–18. This passage tells us of Abraham, who at around a hundred years of age, fully expected (i.e., had hope) that he and Sarah would conceive and have a child. Verse 19 records how Abraham had a steadfast and unwavering hope, even though he knew his body was as good as dead in terms of producing offspring. Verses 17–21 tell us that the basis for his hope was that he had received a promise that this would happen from a God who cannot lie—a God who had all power to do what He said He would do. Verse 20 tells us that he did not lose hope or waver in unbelief, but was strong in faith, giving glory to God.

You see, in this case, Abraham had a true hope because his expectation of good was based on the promises of a God he knew could not and would not lie. His God (and ours) is good, trustworthy, and faithful to keep His promises and powerful enough to fulfill whatever He says.

Verses like these, and so many others, encourage us to have a solid expectation of good because the God who has given us exceedingly great and precious promises is not like us. He is holy—nothing but good.

So it is with every person who has a strong, biblically based hope. It must be based upon, and motivated by, the promises of God.

However, before we can rely upon those promises, we must know them. Many of the people who come to us for counsel are weak in biblical knowledge. It is our privilege to help them discover these promises. They must read them, learn them, and meditate upon them. They must keep their minds filled with them. I like to say that our minds should be marinated in the Word of God.

This means that *we* must know and believe what the Bible teaches about the character of God. We must personally meditate upon the attributes of God and help others to do the same.

Where this becomes practical is in the instance of a person who thinks he's been given more than he can bear. The truth of that thought is that he either does not know or does not believe the truths of 1 Corinthians 10:13 or 2 Corinthians 9:8.

The first says, "No temptation has overtaken you that is not common to man. God is faithful, and he will not let you be tempted beyond your ability, but with the temptation he will also provide the way of escape, that you may be able to endure it."

The second one says, "And God is able to make all grace abound to you, so that having all sufficiency in all things at all times, you may abound in every good work." We serve a big God and it is our responsibility to convey that truth to the ones we seek to inspire to biblical hope.

Other verses that come into play are Romans 8:28, Romans 8:32, Philippians 4:19, and many other verses that contain promises and give reasons for not losing hope. If the counselees seem controlled by fear and anxiety, these are the verses they need to study and meditate upon.

I'll even make a stronger statement. Unless you can inspire a person to have a hope based on the promises and character of God, you will not make much progress in promoting biblical change. Remember—*hope motivates biblical change.*

True biblical hope is only possible for those who have been born again

Unbelievers have no reason for hope. They possess a hope that is vain, false, and dead. They have no valid basis for a *living* hope. That's why we must first ascertain if a person is a believer or not. If our counselee is not, our efforts must be directed towards evangelism before any true offer of help can be made.

This is not only my opinion. We are taught this in the Bible.

* Ephesians 2:1—without Christ we are "dead men walking";
* Ephesians 2:12—unbelievers have no reason for hope;
* 1 Peter 1:3—only those who have been born again have a living hope.

All people suffer—even believers, or perhaps especially believers. Suffering characterizes the lives of believers. Yet we can demonstrate to an unbelieving world that we are more blessed (even in suffering) than unbelievers are at the best of times.

Therefore, since our lives are characterized by suffering, it only makes sense that God would provide instruction for how we are to approach it in a way pleasing to Him. That's why biblical counseling/discipleship is so important.

We all suffer. So, let's learn how to view it from His perspective, how to emerge from it stronger than we were before, and how to help others learn and grow from their experiences. Our pain is not frivolous or capricious. It has purpose. And through every trial, we see at least two positive outcomes—it ultimately results in good for us and glory for God.

Romans 8:16–39 is a passage containing some wonderful promises filled with encouragement and hope for people who are experiencing severe trials. I encourage you to read it, study it, and meditate on its glorious truths.

Verse 18 mentions the sufferings of this present time. Verse 20 says that we live in a created world which causes problems for us because it is subject to futility, constant decay, disintegration, change, and instability. Verse 22 states that the created world in which we live is groaning. (This word, "groaning," comes from a

Greek word used of a person who is in agony, caught in a dreadful situation, and who has no immediate prospect of deliverance.) Verse 23 speaks of the fact that we who live in this created world are also groaning—we experience pain, hardships, violence, agony over our sin and the sin we see in the world, etc. Verses 33–39 expand on the difficulties we experience in this life. They talk about someone bringing charges or accusations against us, about experiencing tribulation, distress, persecution, famine, deprivation, and physical violence.

But in the midst of his realistic description of these things, Paul reminds us that we can have hope! The word *hope* appears in verse 20, three times in verse 24, and once in verse 25. He tells us that in the midst of all these difficulties, we can have a solid expectation of good. And then he tells us why.

1. Verses 18–25: One day, we will be delivered from all suffering, all hardship. One day, every reason for groaning will be gone forever. One day, we will experience nothing but glory in a perfect environment. One day, we will have a redeemed body. He assures us that, when that day comes, we will find it is worth so much more than the suffering we experience now. We won't even consider the difficulties worthy of being compared. When we get to heaven, we will experience the fulfillment of our hope. Our hope then becomes our reality. That understanding of the glorious things that await us in the future motivates us to persevere in the here and now. Therefore, the realization and assurance of future blessings have present-day blessings and promote steadfastness. (See also 2 Cor. 4:16–18, James 1:12 ff, Heb. 11:8–10, 23–27.)
2. Verses 28–30: We are assured that God works everything for good to the ones who believe. God works. God causes. Examine the language Paul uses in these verses. How many times do you find "God causes"? It's because *God causes* that we can truly obtain this hope. In the midst of incredible difficulties, God says we can have an absolute expectation of good. (See also Rom. 5:1–5, Phil. 1:12–14, 20, 2 Cor. 4:7–10, and James 1:2–5.)
3. Verse 32: Paul declares that in the midst of the inevitable

challenges and distresses of life, we can have a confident expectation that God will give us everything we need to handle whatever comes our way. (See also 2 Cor. 12:7–10, Phil. 4:10–13, 2 Cor. 9:8.)

*True biblical hope is based on
an understanding that any good
we experience is a gift of God's pure grace*

Grace is unmerited favor. We did nothing to earn it. God does not owe it to us. We may act like we're entitled to it at times, but the truth is that we are not! God is not obligated to bestow His grace or mercy upon anyone. If He never did any other good thing for us after our salvation, it would still be much more than we deserve.

Yet, God is a good Father and continues to shower us with blessings. Some of these blessings come in the form of trial and tribulation.

In Luke 18:9–14, two men went to the temple. One received hope and went away justified. The other didn't. One thought he deserved God's favor. The other didn't. Instead, he realized he deserved nothing, that God owed him nothing. He was the one who left that day with hope and assurance.

This story clearly teaches us that those who understand their own depravity, sinfulness, and unworthiness are the only people who have any basis for having real hope for good in the present or future. They have come to understand that blessings aren't some kind of payment for the good they do, and that it is only by God's grace that we exist at all. God's grace is the reason we can have this kind of hopeful expectation.

Peter also teaches that hope is connected with God's grace. In 1 Peter 1:13, Peter says, "Therefore, preparing your minds for action, and being sober-minded, set your hope fully on the grace that will be brought to you at the revelation of Jesus Christ."

Now these words aren't addressed to people who are living "the good life" in the worldly sense. He's writing to people struggling with severe problems. Peter knows they are being distressed by various trials, mistreated by their employers, and by their political leaders. He mentions (in 4:12) that these people are experiencing a fiery ordeal. Yet he tells them here in 1:13 to fix their hope *completely* on the grace of God. He encourages them to have hope.

Note what he *doesn't* say. He doesn't tell them to fix their hope on their good works, or their church membership, or their theological understanding, or even their own goodness and faithfulness. No, they are to fix their hope completely upon the grace of God.

Another clear example of this teaching comes from 2 Thessalonians 2:16–17. "Now may our Lord Jesus Christ himself, and God our Father, who loved us and gave us eternal comfort and good hope through grace, comfort your hearts and establish them in every good work and word."

Again, Paul connects this abiding hope with God's grace. We have a good hope because of His grace, not because we know we are so wonderful that we deserve it. (See also 1 Peter 5:6 and Titus 3:3–7.)

In the nineteenth century, Charles H. Spurgeon wrote a book called *All of Grace*. Spurgeon was right. Our relationship with God, from beginning to end and throughout eternity, is all of grace.

From the beginning of our relationship with God, it was His grace which called us, regenerated us, justified us, forgave us, and adopted us into His family. It was His grace that gave us the indwelling Holy Spirit and His grace that gave us the gifts of repentance and faith.

That grace continues to bless us as we journey through this life toward eternity with Him. We stand by grace, serve by grace, worship by grace, and persevere by grace. By His grace, He hears our every prayer. He convicts us of sin. He teaches us. He loves us. He accepts us. And in the end, He will, by His grace, bring us to heaven where we will dwell with Him forever. It's truly all by grace.

What's the point of all this talk about grace? There are several:

- In spite of my own sinfulness, how often I blow it, how often I fail Him, I can still have an expectation of God's help and faithfulness to me because He is full of grace.

- In spite of how undeserving I am, I can know that God will be faithful in forgiving my sins when I confess them. I know that because He is the God of all grace.
- In spite of my unworthiness, I can come to Him knowing that He hears my prayers because of His grace.
- In spite of my own faithlessness, I can know that God will never leave me or forsake me because of His grace.
- In spite of my failings and sinfulness, I can know that God will never give me more than I can bear, but will with every trial provide a way of escape. He is the God of all grace who loves to forgive and save and help and support people who recognize how unworthy they really are.

Because of His grace, I have realized that when professing Christians lack hope, it is either because they don't understand how undeserving and sinful they are, or because they do not understand how gracious God is to people who confess their sins and depend entirely on the Lord Jesus Christ for justification and sanctification. True biblical hope is inseparably connected to the awareness that God's relationship toward His people is totally dependent on His grace. If we recognize and believe that, we have reason for hope.

True biblical hope comes from God implanting and sustaining that hope through the instrumentality of His Word

Romans 15:4 makes the connection between hope and God's Word very clear. "For whatever was written in former days was written for our instruction, that through endurance and through the encouragement of the Scriptures we might have hope."

This truth is brought home repeatedly in Psalm 119:49, which says, "Remember your word to your servant, in which you have made me hope." Verse 74 says, "Those who fear you shall see me and rejoice, because I have hoped in your word." Verse 81 says, "My soul longs for your salvation; I hope in your word." Verse

114 says, "You are my hiding place and my shield; I hope in your word." Verse 147 says, "I rise before dawn and cry for help; I hope in your words."

If we, as counselors, pastors, teachers or parents, are going to inspire a valid attitude of hopefulness, we must make sure that we not only use the Word of God, but use and interpret it properly. We have a responsibility to present a sound interpretation of the Bible when we use it to help other people. That means we must know it thoroughly.

Where is that taught in Scripture? Here are a few examples:

- "Do your best to present yourself to God as one approved, a worker who has no need to be ashamed, rightly handling the word of truth" (2 Tim. 2:15).
- "Now we know that the law is good, if one uses it lawfully" (1 Tim. 1:8).
- "Not many of you should become teachers, my brothers, for you know that we who teach will be judged with greater strictness" (James 3:1).

True biblical hope is generated by biblical thinking

You cannot have a mind filled with unbiblical ideas and opinions and still have a hopeful attitude. If you think unbiblically, you will either lose hope or you will have a false hope that is nothing more than wishful thinking.

To develop and sustain true biblical hope, you *must* think biblically about God, about your situation, about God's purposes for bringing difficulties, about the resources He has given you, about the nature and causes of your problems, about your own personal responsibilities for your actions and responses, about the past and future, and about the biblical solutions to problems. (See Eph. 1:11, Ps. 115:1-8, Rom. 5:2, 2 Tim. 1:7, Gal. 5:19-21, 1 Cor. 10:1-14, Phil. 3:10-14, Ps. 19:7-11.)

True biblical hope is comprehensive in focus

True biblical hope focuses on *what comes next* as well as *the here and now*. In counseling, people come to fix what is broken right now in their lives. But an effective counselor will also provide them with tools to use in the future when conflict or suffering arises (and it will).

In staying comprehensive in our focus, we must take all the facts into consideration. We cannot close our eyes to reality. (We'll discuss this more fully when we get to the chapter on *Inventory*.)

If we are to maintain focus, we must view spiritual realities as more important than material, temporal blessings. If we indeed focus on the spiritual condition, the other usually takes care of itself as a result. (See 1 Tim. 4:8, Phil. 1:29, 2 Cor. 4:16–18, Phil. 1:12.)

True biblical hope is connected to a biblical view of prayer

I cannot stress how important prayer is to the process of counseling and discipleship. We cannot do anything apart from Christ. We must turn to Him and ask Him to cause us to work in the lives of others by His grace.

Prayer is not a formula for getting whatever you want. Many of those who come for counseling think it is. They lose hope when God doesn't respond to their prayers in the way they think He should. God is not a genie in a bottle. He does not change His will for us because we desire something else. So, a right view of prayer is essential in any counseling relationship.

What is a right view of prayer? What is a proper perspective on the way to deal with problems and live the Christian life?

Psalm 127:1–2 says, "Unless the LORD builds the house, those who build it labor in vain. Unless the LORD watches over the city, the watchman stays awake in vain. It is in vain that you rise up early and go late to rest, eating the bread of anxious toil; for he gives to his beloved sleep."

I like this verse because it tells us that it is God who must build, and God who watches. We labor. We strive. But it all comes to nothing unless God makes it happen. It is He who keeps us safe. It is the Lord God who allows us to lay our head on our pillow and fall into a peaceful sleep.

Our reliance upon Him is crucial to the way we live our lives and view our circumstances. Without Him, we can do nothing. That is why the most effective, proactive step we can take is to bring our sorrows to Him in prayer, to trust that He will be with us and carry us through any trial He brings our way.

A person who has a true biblical hope clings to the truths presented in Romans 15:13. "May the God of hope fill you with all joy and peace in believing, so that by the power of the Holy Spirit you may abound in hope." If we are to instill in the people who come to us a true biblical hope, we must continue to point them to the source of true hope—the God of hope.

True biblical hope is not threatened or destroyed by opposition, disagreement or differing points of view

When people lose hope, it causes catastrophic results in their spiritual lives. When they face opposition and disagreement, they lose their confidence. That's what happens when they forget, ignore or become distracted from the fundamental truths we have been discussing. They become forgetful about the promises of God, about the grace of God, about the truths declared in Romans 8. Their thinking becomes more worldly and less biblical. They sometimes go from fervent prayer to no prayer when they develop the unbiblical attitude of "Why should I pray? He doesn't listen to me anyway." Their lives begin to go backwards and finally cave in around them. And they come to us for answers and help.

We must help them rediscover the biblical hope that can be theirs once more. We must point them back to Christ, back to the Bible.

By way of contrast, let's consider the example of people who have a strong hope based on a correct understanding and application of the promises of God. Their minds think biblically and they practice fervent prayer. These things lead to greater hope. It's a cycle of hope.

Our counselees have access to this kind of hope. Once restored, they, too, can have a hope:

- That is steadfast and sure;
- That is coupled with strong conviction and encouragement;
- That will not be shaken by opposition and disagreement;
- That anchors the soul, and is steadfast and sure even while the billows roll;
- That will motivate them to persevere and press forward.

True biblical hope is increased and sustained by the fellowship of other hope-filled believers

This is proven by so many passages in the Bible. I'll name a few.

- "Bear one another's burdens, and so fulfill the law of Christ" (Gal.6:2).
- "Therefore encourage one another and build one another up, just as you are doing" (1 Thess. 5:11).
- "May the Lord grant mercy to the household of Onesiphorus, for he often refreshed me and was not ashamed of my chains" (2 Tim. 1:16).
- "But exhort one another every day, as long as it is called 'today,' that none of you may be hardened by the deceitfulness of sin" (Heb. 3:13).
- "And let us consider how to stir up one another to love and good works, not neglecting to meet together, as is the habit of some, but encouraging one another, and all the more as you see the Day drawing near" (Heb. 10:24–25).

God uses other believers to refresh us, to encourage us, to counsel us, to love us, and to comfort us. We have the opportunity to do that with our counselees, our children, and our brothers and sisters in Christ. We can be the arms of Christ, offering comfort and instruction to those who are suffering. He is not only the God of grace and hope, but also the God of all comfort.

Blessed be the God and Father of our Lord Jesus Christ, the Father of mercies and God of all comfort, who comforts us in all our affliction, so that we may be able to comfort those who are in any affliction, with the comfort with which we ourselves are comforted by God.
(2 Cor. 1:3–4)

How can we do this for those who come to us for help? How can we do this for our children? How can we encourage and comfort one another?

- With words: "Therefore, encourage one another with these words" (1 Thess. 4:18).
- By example: "It was not because we do not have that right, but to give you in ourselves an example to imitate" (2 Thess. 3:9.
- Through deeds: "But be doers of the word, and not hearers only, deceiving yourselves" (James 1:22).

We are privileged to serve our brothers and sisters in these ways, to help them find their hope, and to point them to Christ. This is the subject for our last description of true biblical hope.

True biblical hope is always Christ-centered.

Why is this? Because Christ is the source of biblical hope. He is our Intercessor and Advocate. According to 1 Timothy 1:1, He *is* our hope. "Paul, an apostle of Christ Jesus by command of God our Savior and of Christ Jesus our hope . . ."

According to Colossians 1:27, He is the hope of glory in us. "To them God chose to make known how great among the Gentiles are the riches of the glory of this mystery, which is Christ in you, the hope of glory."

Christ is the founder and perfector of our faith, according to Hebrews 12:1–2. (See also Titus 2:13, 1 John 3:2, 1 Peter 3:15.)

This true biblical hope in Christ is echoed in countless hymns of faith. One of my favorites is *My Hope Rests Firm on Jesus Christ.*

My hope rests firm on Jesus Christ,
He is my only plea;
Though all the world should point and scorn,
His ransom leaves me free, His ransom leaves me free.

My hope sustains me as I strive
And strain towards the goal;
Though I still stumble into sin,
His death paid for it all, His death paid for it all.

My hope provides me with a spur
To help me run this race;
I know my tears will turn to joy
The day I see His face, the day I see His face.

My hope is to be with my Lord,
To know as I am known:
To serve Him gladly all my days
In praise before His throne; in praise before His throne.

Let's begin to summarize. We've discussed many things in this chapter on hope or inspiration. I'll summarize by asking and answering a series of questions:

1. Who needs the most help in developing and maintaining an attitude of hopefulness?
   a. People who are suffering. Peter wrote to people who were going through great suffering. "In this you rejoice, though now for a little while, if necessary, you have been grieved by various trials" (1 Peter 1:6). Peter knew that suffering people need hope, so he reminded them of their reasons for hope in his letters.
   b. People who have lost loved ones. The Thessalonian believers were anxious about those who had died (fallen asleep). Paul knew they needed hope and he gave it to them when he wrote, "But we do not want you to be uninformed, brothers, about those who are asleep, that you may not grieve as others do who have no hope. For

since we believe that Jesus died and rose again, even so, through Jesus, God will bring with him those who have fallen asleep" (1 Thess. 4:13–14).

c. People who are experiencing affliction, fear, difficulties, and hard times. Paul again offered hope and reassurance when he wrote, "Through him we have also obtained access by faith into this grace in which we stand, and we rejoice in hope of the glory of God. More than that, we rejoice in our sufferings, knowing that suffering produces endurance, and endurance produces character, and character produces hope, and hope does not put us to shame, because God's love has been poured into our hearts through the Holy Spirit who has been given to us." (Rom. 5:2–5).

2. What can we do to encourage this attitude of biblical hopefulness in people?
   a. Help them to develop and strengthen a vital relationship with God.
   b. Suggest good, sound books to read about their specific problem(s).
   c. Gently correct their erroneous concepts of God.
   d. Expose them to the attributes of God that are most relevant to the issues at hand.
   e. Impress upon them the potential possibilities for good that may result from working on their issues.
   f. Make them aware of the many resources available to them as believers for handling their problem(s).
   g. Provide information and testimonials from people who have encountered some of the same difficulties, applied godly principles, and survived their circumstances by the grace of God.
   h. Encourage them to pray fervently to the One who is sovereign over all things. Pray with and for them, that God will produce and sustain an attitude of hopefulness.
   i. Encourage them to identify their specific problem and implement a specific biblical procedure to help resolve it.

j. Encourage them to avoid continued association with others who are negative and hopeless, and spend more time with people who possess true biblical hope and joy.

k. Make sure they're reading and studying Scriptures relevant to their situation.

l. Encourage them to initiate daily quiet time or devotions, starting their day out by recognizing Him.

m. Help them learn to take charge of their thought life—talking to themselves instead of listening to themselves.

n. Assign study assignments that are designed to instruct and inspire them as they pertain to their particular issues.

I know this is a long list, but that's a good thing. It gives you many ways to come alongside the ones you are trying to help.

True biblical hope—or what I'm calling inspiration—is vital to the ultimate well-being of the counselee. Instead of being based on mere feelings, true biblical hope is based on the truths contained in the Word of God. Biblical change cannot take place without it.

4

Inventory

This chapter continues the discussion of the key elements of biblical change or counseling. Thus far we have considered the elements of establishing *Involvement* and encouraging *Inspiration*. Now it's time to move on to the third "I" of effective biblical counseling/discipling which is *Inventory*. In this chapter, I'd like to

- Explain why biblical counselors should be concerned about being thorough in the data gathering aspect of counseling;
- Define different kinds of data an effective biblical counselor should seek;
- Give some "how to" suggestions for obtaining this important information.

Why is it important to take a good inventory in the counseling setting?

Actually, there's not a single reason for doing this—no, there are *many* reasons to do it. Gathering data is an art if done correctly. We'll get to the "how-to" later, but let's discuss the "why" in this section.

For one thing, if we keep the counselee's benefit firmly in mind, we will want to be thorough for *his* good. The more thorough we are in gathering data, the more we will understand the whole situation, and the better we can guide him through the process.

For our counselees, it will help to more fully understand the nature and causes of their problems. If we fully comprehend their problems, we will be able to frame them in biblical language—and once we do that, we can bring to bear the Scriptures designed to overcome such problems. The ones seeking help begin to understand how relevant the Bible is to their own life and difficulties and so they gain greater respect for the Word of God. They begin to see that the Bible really does speak to their deepest issues. Once this occurs, many become excited to learn more about the Bible's explanations and solutions.

Data gathering encourages counselees to be cooperative. If they realize how important this step is for them, they will be less likely to hold back on sharing their story. They become more willing participants of the counseling sessions.

Additionally, this back and forth cluster of questions and answers builds the kind of *involvement* so necessary to effective counseling. It adds to the counselor's credibility which, in turn, allows the counselee to have more confidence and *inspiration* (hope) as he approaches his problem(s). Through this gathering of data, the counselee can focus on major issues without lecturing or preaching from the counselor. The facts become obvious through this process and the counselee's comfort level grows.

This increased level of comfort between the counselor and the counselee allows the counselee to lower his shield and may even lead to a conviction of his own sins. Once this awareness takes place, it could lead to genuine repentance.

I hope you are beginning to see how interwoven these key elements become in the counseling setting. They are designed for the good of those who seek our counsel.

Yet, though they are designed for the counselee's best benefit, they offer a tremendous advantage for the counselor, as well. These key elements make us more effective in helping others, which is our goal, after all,

How does obtaining a thorough inventory help us accomplish that goal? Asking the right kind of questions will

• Help us comprehend the true nature and causes of the problem(s). Just as a doctor needs to gather the right data to make a diagnosis, so also we need data to correctly "diagnose" the counselee's problem;

- Allow us to figure out the best way to relate to our counselee;
- Show us, more specifically, the kind of help that is needed in each case;
- Prevent us from offering the wrong kind of counsel (like the counsel Job's friends gave, for example);
- Enable us to teach without lecturing or preaching;
- Allow us greater control of the session.

In teaching and training counselors in biblical counseling, I often use this acronym to describe the kinds of data counselors should seek to gather. It explains the areas of information we need to investigate. We will use the acronym PREACH+D to help us remember the kinds of data we should want to gather.

P—Physical
R—Resources and Relationships
E—Emotional
A—Actions
C—Conceptual or Cognitive
D—Historical Desires

Let's take the acronym apart and examine each area and why they are important to effective biblical counseling.

P—Physical

Many times, we are eager to jump right into a counselee's problems without gathering data on this important area. Why is his physical condition important to the process?

1. What is happening in the physical realm may be the *circumstantial* cause of his non-physical problems.
2. What is happening in the physical realm may provide helpful clues in identifying what is happening in the non-physical realm.

Certainly, this is an area a counselor may feel uncomfortable addressing as it gets very personal. But a calm, gentle approach will ease any awkwardness for the counselee and may provide clues and answers an effective counselor can use to make that crucial diagnosis.

The areas we should investigate are: sleep patterns, diet, activity level, illnesses, physical handicaps, work patterns, drug use, dress (attire), hygienic issues, facial expressions, body posture, and general appearance.

R—Resources

After addressing the problems discovered in the physical assessment, we must explore the resources our counselee has access to. These resources may be financial, intellectual, educational, spiritual, theological, social, familial, and/or circumstantial.

Why would an effective counselor want to investigate this area? We'll look to the Bible for the answer. "Two are better than one, because they have a good reward for their toil. For if they fall, one will lift up his fellow. But woe to him who is alone when he falls and has not another to lift him up! Again, if two lie together, they keep warm, but how can one keep warm alone? And though a man might prevail against one who is alone, two will withstand him—a threefold cord is not quickly broken" (Eccl. 4:9–12).

So the primary reason is for support of the counselee. (See also Gal. 6:2–3, 1 Thess. 5:11, Prov. 18:24.) We must understand the strengths and weaknesses he is drawing upon. Having a firm support system can be a terrific advantage for someone going through trials. At times, we may need to show him how to access those resources, but that can be an ongoing process during each counseling session.

What are the particular areas we need to investigate in this *Resource* category? We need to find out the following:

- Whether or not he is a genuine Christian;
- The depth of his relationship with God;
- His devotional practices
- How much or how little he knows about the Word;

- What resources his family provides;
- What his social resources (friendships) are;
- What kind of financial resources are available;
- What his past experiences have been;
- What his educational resources are;
- What theological resources he has access to.

This information answers the question of how much support the counselee has. Can he rely on their family, friends, or church to provide encouragement and support through the counseling process? Does the counselee have resources he is yet to find out about? Can we facilitate an introduction to help him and reinforce the instruction he hears from the counselor?

E—Emotional

Some counselors want to focus entirely on this emotional aspect, whereas others ignore it completely. How does an effective counselor approach this area of investigation?

The Bible has much to say about emotions. In Proverbs 10 alone, we find gladness, sorrow, hatred, love, pleasure, desire, and joy. And that's just one chapter in the Bible.

God's Word is replete with all kinds of emotions. If a person can feel it, it will be somewhere in Scripture. The Bible depicts the full range of human emotions—from pleasurable and righteous to painful and sinful.

In the Bible, emotions are usually, but not always, paired with descriptions of sinfulness. Several biblical passages have lists of sins and many of our emotions have made those lists. For instance, Galatians 5:19–21 states: "Now the works of the flesh are evident: sexual immorality, impurity, sensuality, idolatry, sorcery, enmity, strife, jealousy, fits of anger, rivalries, dissensions, divisions, envy, drunkenness, orgies, and things like these." There is lots of emotion in that list. (See also Rom. 1:28–31, Eph. 4:31–32, Col. 3:8.)

In addition to these lists, the Bible also teaches us about people who sin. And their sins usually began with their emotions. Some biblical examples are Adam and Eve (Gen. 3), Cain (Gen. 4), Esau

(Gen. 27), King Saul (1 Sam. 18), and King David (2 Sam. 11). I could go on and on with biblical examples of men and women sinning as a result of allowing their emotions to guide their thoughts and actions.

I have a dear friend who studied with a mentor who constantly focused on the intellect instead of her emotions. When she questioned him about it one day, he told her that she knew how to *feel* but obviously no one had taught her to *think biblically*. She agreed. He told her, "Emotions are God-given. They are wonderful as long as you control them, and they don't control you."

That's the problem. Most of our sins are wrapped up in emotion. When we follow them instead of the wisdom God gave us in His Word, we are bound for trouble. We must show people to rely on God's principles instead of their "gut." Most of the problems we face with our counselees are steeped in emotion—and the resulting sin. It is vitally important that we investigate this crucial area.

The Bible makes it clear that our feelings influence our thinking, our attitudes, and our actions. For instance, Proverbs 12:25 states: "Anxiety in a man's heart weighs him down, but a good word makes him glad." (See also Prov. 14:30, Prov. 17:22, Eph. 4:26–27.)

In a way, we can say that our emotions are indicators. We are to pay attention to them because we know where they can lead. Our counselees may not understand that, yet. We must teach them. Our feelings function as smoke detectors alerting us to danger.

As Peter wrote in 1 Peter 5:8, "Be sober-minded, be watchful. Your adversary the devil prowls around like a roaring lion, seeking someone to devour. Resist him, firm in your faith, knowing that the same kinds of suffering are being experienced by your brotherhood throughout the world."

Satan is looking for a way into our hearts. Uncontrolled emotions make a great way for him to gain entrance. (See also James 4:1–8.) The good news here is that Christians, through the power of the Holy Spirit, have the ability to control their emotions and follow and obey the principles God sets out for them in His Word.

A—Actions

Certainly, this is a major area of investigation. In most cases, someone's actions are the catalyst bringing a hurting person to a counselor—either his own actions or the actions of others.

God is certainly concerned about our actions. James 1:22 provides one example of that. "But be doers of the word, and not hearers only, deceiving yourselves." (See also Luke 11:28, Eph. 2:8–10, Titus 3:8–11.) Our actions, good or evil, are of great concern to the Lord and therefore should be of great concern to an effective biblical counselor.

Just as people's emotions and thoughts can produce actions, their actions also influence their thoughts and feelings. They can have quite an impact, in fact.

The Bible indicates that a person's actions and reactions demonstrate the reality or falsehood of his profession of faith. Find out what fruit is produced by the one in need of help.

Those actions and reactions also reveal what is going on in that person's heart. We can't look into the heart of a man, like Christ could. That's why it's important for us to investigate and review their actions. Their actions and responses will give us the best glimpse into what is inside their heart.

What areas should we investigate?

- What a person is doing that he should not be doing;
- What a person is doing that he should be doing;
- What a person is doing in the area of his speech and how that impacts his problem(s);
- How a person is behaving in his family relationships that may violate God's Word;
- What a person is doing in the area of sex that may impact the issues he brings to us;
- What a person does in the area of his work;
- How a person responds in his relationships with other people;
- What he does in the area of finances and material things;
- What about his actions in reference to the stewardship of his body (sleep, exercise, eating, overwork, carelessness,

not taking necessary medications, illegal drug use, physical abuse, food abuse, alcohol abuse, etc.);

- What the counselee does in the area of recreational activities (reading materials, television, sports, movies, Internet activities, pornography, music);
- What actions he makes in regard to the area of worship and devotions;
- How he uses his time or abilities.

This covers a broad area. However, we need to understand our counselee's actions to give him the most specific types of help and instruction. It is for his good that we investigate.

C—Conceptual, Cognitive

This area pertains to thoughts, attitudes, perspectives, and interpretations. The Bible gives us many reasons to explore this important area.

- "For he is like one who is inwardly calculating" (Prov. 23:7).
- "As in water face reflects face, so the heart of man reflects the man" (Prov. 27:19).
- "For the word of God is living and active, sharper than any two-edged sword, piercing to the division of soul and of spirit, of joints and of marrow, and discerning the thoughts and intentions of the heart" (Heb. 4:12).
- "The LORD saw that the wickedness of man was great in the earth, and that every intention of the thoughts of his heart was only evil continually" (Gen. 6:5).
- "Search me, O God, and know my heart! Try me and know my thoughts! And see if there be any grievous way in me, and lead me in the way everlasting!" (Ps. 139:23–24).

Apparently, we are wise counselors if we can assess this important area of the thoughts of the heart. And yes, when we detect something grievous there, we can help by leading in the way of the Lord.

What are some of the conceptual areas a biblical counselor

should investigate? There are too many to name completely! And you will find some crossover from the other areas we've discussed. But here are a few that I believe to be most important.

First, we should find out what they think and believe about God. Then explore how they think of themselves, about their priorities, about their standard for right and wrong. We should gather information about their values and theological issues, about how they think they should be treated by others, and how they should treat others.

We must challenge them to identify how they believe change occurs, about their personal responsibility, about past and present circumstances as well as how they view their future. We must ascertain what hurting people view as the cause of their problem and what they believe the solution to be.

One important piece of information, which is often overlooked, is for us to find out what they expect or want from counseling. What are their expectations for what we can provide for them?

Their answers will provide additional clues to what the core problems are. When we understand this, we can tailor our instruction to the core. An effective counselor is not satisfied with helping overcome one problem. If the core problems are not addressed, the counselee will find himself in this problem repeatedly. We must help him overcome the core problem.

It's like the old analogy of peeling an onion. Talking with a counselee reveals a layer of the onion. With questions designed to reveal the thoughts of the heart, more layers are peeled away until, at last, the core of the onion is exposed. Sometimes this is all that is needed to begin true biblical change.

You would think the counselee would be aware of the core problem but may be unwilling to reveal it at first. My experience has taught me that the counselee is sometimes the last person to figure out what the core problem is—and is utterly surprised when it's revealed!

H—Historical

....

Again, the Bible supports delving into this important area of inventory. For instance, Proverbs 22:24–25 says, "Make no friendship with a man given to anger, nor go with a wrathful man, lest you learn his ways and entangle yourself in a snare." A person's history is vital to understanding his problems.

The situation described in 1 Corinthians 10:1–11 is also a good case in point. After detailing the sins and idolatry of the past, Paul says, "Now these things happened to them as an example, but they were written down for our instruction, on whom the end of the ages has come" (1 Cor. 10:11).

Almost the entire Old Testament provides a history of the people of God—the nation of Israel. It is important to have a cohesive understanding of the Bible to know this detailed history—how things fit together in the big picture.

So also, it's important to figure out how things fit together in the big picture of our counselee's past.

What areas should be investigated? Here are a few:

- Parental example/instruction/discipline;
- Previous trauma, difficulties, and how those things were dealt with and resolved;
- What are some of the most pleasant, enjoyable, satisfying, and rewarding experiences the person has had?
- Who are the main players in his current conflict?
- What has happened that led to the problem?
- What is the timeline for these actions?
- How did the person respond to these circumstances?
- Has the counselee ever been through similar problems in the past?
- Identify patterns or themes that may occur;
- Discover what your counselee looks for in his friends;
- Identify unfinished business from the past (things that still need to be done to clear up past sinful actions or reactions);
- Continue to promote *involvement* and *inspiration* through this interview process.

D—Desire

This brings us to the last letter in the acronym PREACHD. Understanding the counselee's desires is tremendously important. The desires of their hearts reveal much about their behaviors and expectations in many areas.

And yes, the Bible provides reasons why it is important to delve into this personal area. It gives example after example of events where actions or sins take place as a result of the desires of the heart. Here are a few:

- "But each person is tempted when he is lured and enticed by his own desire. Then desire when it has conceived gives birth to sin, and sin when it is fully grown brings forth death. Do not be deceived, my beloved brothers" (James 1:14–16).
- "Now the works of the flesh are evident: sexual immorality, impurity, sensuality, idolatry, sorcery, enmity, strife, jealousy, fits of anger, rivalries, dissensions, division, envy, drunkenness, orgies, and things like these" (Gal. 5:19–21a).
- "So when the woman saw that the tree was good for food, and that it was a delight to the eyes, and that the tree was to be desired to make one wise, she took of its fruit and ate, and she also gave some to her husband who was with her, and he ate" (Gen. 3:6).
- "What causes quarrels and what causes fights among you? Is it not this, that your passions are at war within you? You desire and do not have, so you murder. You covet and cannot obtain, so you fight and quarrel" (James 4:1–2).
- "For all that is in the world—the desires of the flesh and the desires of the eyes and pride in possessions—is not from the Father but is from the world" (1 John 2:16).

I don't think anyone would argue with this fact: sinful desires lead to sin. But the positive is also true. Godly desires lead to godly behaviors and attitudes. It's important that we assess this important area so we will better discern the person's strengths and weaknesses.

Our desires dictate what we do every day. The very acts of getting up and going to bed reflect our desires. Our desires determine how hard we work, how much time we spend with the Lord, how fit we are, how much we eat, how we respond to our spouse and to our children. Desires direct our everyday actions, responses, and relationships.

What areas of desire (motivation) should an effective counselor investigate? Once again, there are many.

For instance, what does the person really desire that is motivating thoughts and/or behavior? What do they get out of this behavior? What do they expect to gain from this behavior?

Do they feel deprived of something they desire? What are they *not* getting that they want more than they want to please God? What do they think would have to happen or change for them to be happy, satisfied, and/or successful? Who are they most interested in pleasing? Themselves? Or God? Who or what is ruling their life?

How are we to gather all this inventory of data?

In addition to considering the questions of why we are to gather this data, and what kind of data to obtain, we must also consider *how* to ask questions designed to acquire this *inventory*.

I hope to show that to you in this section. Consider the following diagrams.

The first thing we need to understand is how to ask proper questions. Proper questions are asked in a thoughtful, considerate, and gracious manner. Colossians 4:6 says, "Let your speech always be gracious, seasoned with salt, so that you may know how you ought to answer each person." (See also Eph. 4:29, Prov. 16:21, 24, Prov. 15:1, 4.)

The next thing to consider is the importance of asking open-ended questions. Closed-ended questions have *yes* or *no* answers, which do not lend themselves to any extrapolation. Using questions beginning with *what, when, where, how,* or *why* allows the counselee to open up more.

Inventorying the Person and His Problems

The counselee's world and life may be divided into two main areas—outer and inner

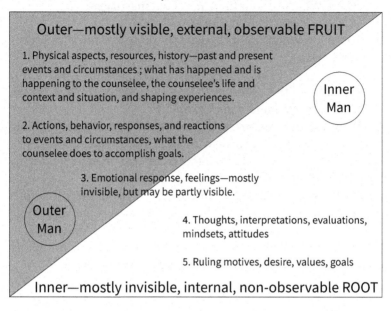

Outer—mostly visible, external, observable FRUIT

1. Physical aspects, resources, history—past and present events and circumstances ; what has happened and is happening to the counselee, the counselee's life and context and situation, and shaping experiences.

2. Actions, behavior, responses, and reactions to events and circumstances, what the counselee does to accomplish goals.

3. Emotional response, feelings—mostly invisible, but may be partly visible.

4. Thoughts, interpretations, evaluations, mindsets, attitudes

5. Ruling motives, desire, values, goals

Inner Man

Outer Man

Inner—mostly invisible, internal, non-observable ROOT

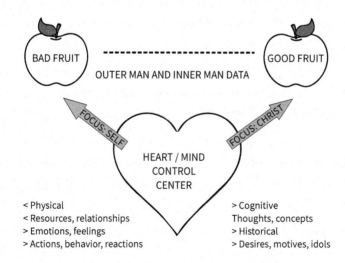

BAD FRUIT — — — — — — — — — — — — GOOD FRUIT

OUTER MAN AND INNER MAN DATA

FOCUS: SELF   FOCUS: CHRIST

HEART / MIND
CONTROL
CENTER

< Physical
< Resources, relationships
> Emotions, feelings
> Actions, behavior, reactions

> Cognitive
Thoughts, concepts
> Historical
> Desires, motives, idols

Jeremiah 17:5-10; Mark 7:14-23; Ephesians 4:22-24;
Colossians 3:1-17; Galatians 5:16-26; James 1:12-15; Genesis 6:5

- *Closed*: Do you want to get married?
- *Open*: What are your thoughts about marriage?
- *Closed*: Do you love your husband?
- *Open*: How would you describe your relationship with your husband?

Do you see the difference? One potentially shuts a person down. The other opens a person up.

We follow in the footsteps of Jesus when we ask soul-searching questions. Even a quick read through the Gospel accounts of Christ will reveal that He used this technique often and expertly. We can rightly call Jesus the greatest question asker!

Why was it so important to Him to ask questions? He didn't do it to obtain information, because He knew what was in the heart of a man. Perhaps, then, He did it to make people think, to promote conviction, to engage them in conversation, to solidify their conviction, or as a means of teaching them.

For us, as we counsel, I believe we should ask questions for some of these same reasons. Yet, there's another primary reason for asking questions properly—so that we can obtain information. We are not Jesus. We cannot see into a person's heart. We ask questions to find out what's in there.

Proverbs 18:2 says, "A fool takes no pleasure in understanding, but only in expressing his opinion." Let us not be foolish. We are not there to talk about our own opinions or beliefs or to make assumptions. We must make sure we seek to gain understanding of the person and his situation. We must put in the work and not be sloppy about gathering such information.

If we are to be effective biblical counselors, we must heed the teaching of Proverbs 18:13. "If one gives an answer before he hears, it is his folly and shame." Job's counselors answered before they listened, so they hurt rather than helped Job. They serve as examples of what *not* to do.

As we counsel, we must be careful that we don't function the way those "friends" did with Job. We must adhere to the instruction of Proverbs 18:15, which says, "An intelligent heart acquires knowledge, and the ear of the wise seeks knowledge."

As I said previously, we don't go into a counseling setting knowing everything about a person's past or present, about his thoughts, emotions, desires, circumstances, and resources. That's why it's important to at least know something about these issues if we are going to offer wise, helpful, God-honoring counsel.

Another factor in asking proper questions is that they should be asked progressively or contextually. What does that mean?

It means that each question we ask should be based on information acquired from the answer to former questions— they should flow out of the former answer. Asking questions like this keeps the conversation on track and prevents long periods of storytelling, which can prove to be a waste of time and might allow the person to pursue rabbit trails, getting off the subject. Therefore, our questions should provide continuity and movement through the conversation.

Our questions should connect the dots—providing a flow from one point to another. This gives the counselee more confidence that we are headed in a certain direction because we understand the issues involved.

Asking good questions has another benefit to the counselee. They encourage personal evaluation. Exploring these areas may lead him to make self-discoveries which can be extremely beneficial—maybe more so than if he is merely told.

Getting *really* practical

My desire in teaching and counseling is to be practical in my approach. These previous sections are practical. But now I want to get *really* practical. Through all the years I've spent counseling hurting people, I have developed many, many helpful questions in getting them to talk, and retrieving relevant clues as they speak.

I'd like to share some of those questions with you about each of the areas we covered in the PREACHD acronym. We'll start at the beginning, and I'll give you five questions per area.

Physical:

- Generally speaking, how would you describe your present and past physical health?
- What is it you like or dislike about yourself physically?
- How would you describe your eating habits?
- Tell me about your daily intake of beverages containing caffeine.
- What kind of physical activities do you do on a regular basis?

Resource:

- Tell me about the most important persons in your life and why he or she is so important to you.
- Share with me the relationship that give you the greatest joy and the ones that give the most sadness or heartache.
- What do you usually do when you have a problem?
- Tell me who you feel most comfortable sharing your private thoughts and feelings with.
- Tell me about your relationship with God—how it began, how it has developed, how important it is, where God fits into the total picture of your life, and what you are doing to strengthen your relationship with Him.

Emotional:

- What emotions do you most frequently experience?
- If you were able to change anything about yourself emotionally, what would you want to change?
- Give me a few examples of times when you were really. . . .
- When do you feel the happiest? And about what?
- How do you feel about what is happening in your life right now?

Action:

- As you look back over your life, what are some of the things you have done that you think are really worthwhile?

- What are some of the things you wish you could undo?
- As you look at your life right now, what are some of the things you think you are doing that are right? And the ones that are wrong?
- Tell me about some of the ways you see yourself growing as a Christian.
- Tell me about some of the ways you have helped other people, or ways you've been a hindrance to them.

Cognitive/Conceptual:

- What do you see as your most pressing problem?
- What do you think about the way you have handled the problem?
- Describe how you think a person or a couple should make decisions.
- Where do you think God fits into all that is happening right now?
- What do you think God's solution to this problem would be?

Historical:

- When did you first begin to experience this problem?
- What was happening in your life when. . . .
- Tell me about your relationship with the Lord over the years—its high points and low points.
- What situations in life do you find most difficult to handle?
- What past experiences in life are hardest for you to let go of?

Desire:

- What brings out the worst in you? The best?
- What are your goals, expectations, or intentions?
- What is your greatest source of happiness?
- What do you most fear or worry about?
- When you are pressured or tense, where do you turn? What do you do or think about?

Now, if I give you good examples to follow, let me also give you some practices regarding proper questions to avoid. Like I said, I've been doing this a long time and have learned from past mistakes. In giving you this list, I hope I can help you avoid making the same mistakes in your own counseling or parenting. You should avoid:

- Getting carried away with your own curiosity (especially if it has nothing to do with the issue at hand);
- Asking questions in machine-gun style;
- Asking leading questions designed to lock the counselee into giving you the answer you have already decided you want to get;
- Becoming satisfied with vague, abstract answers. You want specific, not general, answers to your questions;
- Allowing the person to shift the blame, to make excuses, or to gossip about others.

Positive Listening Techniques

"Anyone can listen," you might say. "Why do I need instruction on listening? That's a no-brainer."

The truth of the matter is that most people are not good listeners. Here are some tips I'd like to leave you with in the area of positive listening techniques.

When I say listening techniques, I'm talking about both verbal and non-verbal communication. Non-verbal cues can sometimes give more information than words. So, watch your counselee's expressions and his body language. Observe his clothing, gestures, posture, where he sits, any signs of nervousness, indifference, or hopelessness. Listen to the tone of his voice and to volume changes in it. Note the eye contact (both with you and with his spouse if the other party is present).

Listen to what he's telling you. As well as listening for what he *does* say, listen for what he *doesn't* say.

Listen for any anger, defensiveness, self-pity, discouragement, hopelessness, blame-shifting, evasiveness, annoyance, victim mentality, exaggerations, and generalities.

Note repeated words, phrases, or experiences.

Listen carefully for the person's working theology—his view of God—as well as for unbiblical thinking, especially about the nature and causes of his problems.

Listen for indications explaining why the hurting person has come to you at this time, and try to get a sense of his expectations of the counseling experience.

As well as practicing positive listening techniques, avoid falling into these familiar traps:

- Don't constantly or unnecessarily interrupt.
- Don't allow your mind to wander.
- Don't think about what you're going to say next and miss what he's saying now.
- Don't do distracting things (like looking at your phone or watch, answering a call, or picking at your clothes).
- Don't jump to conclusions.

In addition to verbal questions and answers, some counselors make good use of other methods to gather information. One such method is to have their counselees fill out a personal data inventory (PDI) sheet. Another method is to observe the person interacting outside the counseling setting—for example, with his spouse, with family members, with friends, in church, at athletic events, group gatherings, etc.

Another means of gathering data is to pay attention to how your counselee does the homework assignments you give. Review it with him so he knows he will be held accountable. Did he do a thorough job with it or just enough to get by? Did he take it seriously? What did he think about the homework?

Another way of obtaining information is to ask your counselee to keep a daily journal of times when he experiences his presenting problem. Go over these events with him.

Don't forget to keep notes on each counseling session you have. Record important statements, observations, information, and insights acquired. Keep track of the Scriptures discussed and the homework given. Before the next session, review your notes and write out issues you want to discuss and areas in which you would like to gain more information. Being a good, effective biblical counselor requires more than just sharing your wisdom with someone else. It involves *work*. It involves *prayer*. It involves *seeking another's highest good*. Just as you expect the counselee to complete the homework you give him, so also you must do your own homework to increase the effectiveness of your counsel. Remember, you're doing this to the glory of God. Be thorough. Be kind. Be wise.

Now let's move on to the next "I" of biblical counseling— *Interpretation*.

5

Interpretation

What I'm calling the eight "I"s is the model or paradigm that I use for the practice of biblical counseling. They describe what we must do to help people put off ungodly patterns of thinking and living, and put on godly patterns. We've covered *Involvement, Inspiration,* and *Inventory.* It's time to turn our attention to the next of the "I"s—*Interpretation.*

Interpretation involves promoting true biblical change by analyzing and organizing the information we have gleaned in the inventory process so we can accurately identify in biblical terms the nature and causes of the person's problem. Only then can we convincingly explain this to the one turning to us for counsel.

This chapter explains a process by which the information we've obtained may be analyzed biblically so we may accurately understand the nature and causes of the counselee's problem(s). After we have arrived at a conclusion, we may then go on to provide accurate, helpful, and appropriate biblical instruction.

What do I find in the Bible to support this important step? There are many examples, but I'll give you two.

1. The first example is in Luke 10:38–42. This is the famous discussion between Jesus and Martha.
    a. Facts/circumstances (vv. 38–39)
    b. Martha's response/interpretation (v. 40)
    c. Our Lord's interpretation (vv. 41–42)

2. The second example is in Luke 24:13-26. This is the famous discourse between Jesus and the disciples along the road to Emmaus.
   a. Facts/circumstances (vv. 13-18)
   b. Disciples' response (vv. 19-21)
   c. Our Lord's interpretation (vv. 25-26)

Let's examine some case studies to see how this comes into play in a counseling session. Or does it?

Mike came in for counseling, stating that his problem was church membership. When asked to explain, he said, "I'm single, twenty-five years old, and I attend two different churches. I think I should become a member of one and devote my energies there. But I can't decide which one to join. I've been praying for guidance for a long time, but the Lord hasn't shown me which church I should join. I still don't know which one to join. What do you think?"

You ask, "What have you done to discover the Lord's will in this matter?"

"I've mostly prayed a lot that He would just show me what to do."

"That's fine," you say, "but how have you expected Him to reveal His will to you?"

"Well, the normal way, I suppose. You know, by little signs and feelings. I want to really know inside where I should be and have a real peace about it."

Effectively counseling Mike will require gathering data. What data do we already have from what Mike has said? What other information would you want to gather? For instance, what information might you want to learn in terms of the physical area, relationship, emotions, actions, concepts, history, and desires?

Effectively counseling Mike will require doing some inventory work, but it will require doing more than gathering data. It will also require putting that information under the microscope and doing some accurate and biblical interpretation of that data. It will require answering the questions, "Is Mike's problem simply a matter of not knowing how to discern God's will in reference to joining a church? Or is it more than that?" It will involve identifying the various possibilities that may be involved in Mike's difficulty in making a decision about which church to join and then deciding which of those possibilities is involved in Mike's indecisiveness.

Let's look at another example.

> Gus comes to you stating that he needs help because, as he puts it, "Feelings of inferiority have made me physically ill and generally impotent as a person. I've tried to live the way I hear you saying a Christian should live, but I just can't because I feel so inferior. I'm a failure in so many areas of life. It makes me tense around people and I just don't think it's fair that God made other people who are so much more gifted and successful and confident than I am. When I'm around people, I find myself freezing up and getting very nervous. I'm not doing well in school and I'm afraid I will flunk out. I'm not a quitter or anything, but I just can't live and function the way the Bible says a Christian should function. I want to, but I just can't. If I just had more ego strength and a better self-image, I might be able to do so. Please help me find some self-esteem so I can develop a better self-image."

If you're going to effectively counsel Gus, you will need to do several things. First, you need to establish involvement, practice inspiration, and gather data (inventory). Gus has already given you some initial information. What data do we already have from what Gus has said? What other information would you want or need to gather? For instance, what data might you want to gather in terms of the physical area of his life, relationships, emotions, actions, concepts, history, and desires? If you do not gather this additional information, you may be guilty of giving merely pharisaical or behavioristic counseling.

To counsel Gus effectively, we will have to do more than gather PREACHD data. We will also need to make an accurate interpretation of the nature and cause of Gus's problems. We need to reveal his core problem and be able to discuss this with him or the counsel we give him will go nowhere. We must put the information we acquire from Gus under the microscope and do some accurate and biblical interpretation. We need to be able to answer the questions "Is Gus's problem really a matter of his lacking ego strength? Is it really a matter Gus failing because of the way God has made him? Is he really failing because of his low self-esteem and bad self-image?" Counseling him will involve identifying the various possibilities that may be involved in what is happening in his life, and then explaining them in a way that Gus understands. At that point, we can address his problems in a biblical way.

I could go on and on with these examples, but I won't. Instead, let me explain how to make an accurate and biblical interpretation of the nature and causes of the problems we encounter. Here are some generic interpretative guidelines or steps.

1. As you engage in the inventory phase of counseling, you should prayerfully compare what you discover from the counselee with the standard of God's Word. As you gather data, you should be comparing:
    a. The person's behavioral responses with the standard of God's Word to see where and how they are unbiblical.
    b. The person's emotional responses with the standard of God's Word.
    c. The person's thoughts, attitudes, and interpretations with the standard of God's Word.
    d. The person's desires, values, expectations, and motivations with the standard of God's Word.

2. Carefully and prayerfully take the information you've gathered and look for existing themes or patterns you see emerging, rather than just focusing on one issue at a time. This means you must be on the lookout for typical responses in the life of the person you're counseling.
    a. As I attempt to determine whether a person has typical responses, I have found that asking myself and the counselee the following questions can be very revealing.
        i. Does the data indicate that there is a particular time

of day or a place when or where the problem is most likely to occur?

  ii. Does the data indicate that there are typical emotional responses in certain situations or when certain things occur?

  iii. Does the data indicate that there are typical expectations, desires, longings, and demands the person has of certain people or situations?

 b. Another useful tool in this is having the person keep a daily journal in which he records information relevant to what has brought him for counseling.

 c. Another helpful way of discovering unbiblical patterns is through the use of a sentence completion form. The counselee is asked to complete the sentence. For example, "I get nervous when _____." Or, "I would be happier if only _____."

3. Another important factor for making an accurate and biblically informed interpretation involves taking the information you've collected and making sure you label and describe the person's problems in biblical terms.

 a. This means you should use biblical words and categories instead of psychological ones. It is not useful and can actually be harmful to use psychological labels when doing biblical counseling.

 b. For example, instead of "weaknesses," speak in terms of sin. Instead of "overeating," speak in terms of gluttony. Instead of "having a bit of a drinking problem," use the term drunkenness.

4. To make an accurate biblical interpretation of the nature and cause of a person's problems, we should take the information, put it on the witness stand, and make it answer some questions.

 a. One question would be: What biblical categories could be used to describe the person I'm counseling?

  i. Is the person a believer or a nonbeliever?

  ii. Is the person mature or immature?

      iii. Where would this person fit in the 1 Thessalonians 5:14 categories of unruly, fainthearted, discouraged, or weak?

      iv. Where would this person fit in the Proverbs 10:1, 8 categories of foolish *versus* wise?

  b. What does the data indicate about this person's understanding of biblical change? Does he desire biblical change?

  c. What does the data indicate about possible complicating or compounding factors?

  d. What does the data indicate about possible organic factors? (See below.)

  e. What does the data indicate about the best way to approach the counselee/disciple/child?

  f. What does the data indicate about the person's greatest need at this point?

  g. What does the data indicate about why the person has not resolved the problem until now? Why is he only now coming to us for help?

  h. What does the data indicate about what the person wants or expects from counseling?

5. We must take the information we've accumulated and prayerfully study it to identify what is going on in the person's heart.

  a. This important factor is one we emphasized earlier.

  b. As we seek to understand the nature and cause of a person's problems, it is important for us to identify what the data tells us about what is going on in the person's heart. We must study the data to identify what the person's ruling motives are. We need to analyze the data to discern who or what the person is worshiping.

Biblically speaking, the heart is the mission control center of our lives—Proverbs 4:23, Hebrews 4:12, Mark 7:21–23. The Bible teaches that our attitudes, feeling, and behavior are ruled and driven by our beliefs and desires. The Bible teaches that we were made to worship and, at every point in our lives, we either worship and serve the true God or a false god. This means that:

WHEN WE WORSHIP THE TRUE GOD	WHEN WE WORSHIP A FALSE GOD
We have godly desires.	We have worldly desires.
We fear God.	We fear man.
We live to please God.	We live to please self/other people.

What to make of bizarre, weird behaviors

I'd like to end this chapter on inventory with this. Too many times, counselors—even biblical ones—tend to throw up their hands when confronted with someone presenting with weird and bizarre behaviors. I have personally dealt with such people.

One person comes to mind who came to the counseling session draped in aluminum foil, wearing an aluminum foil hat. She was so afraid of everything, she trusted no one. Her paranoia had chased off her husband and her friends. She had been diagnosed with schizophrenia.

Others had thrown their hands up and passed her on to someone else—maybe a psychiatrist who "knows how to treat people with this diagnosis." I didn't pass her on to someone else. I counseled her. I asked questions. I demonstrated *involvement* with her. I offered *inspiration* to her. She came to trust me and to feel safe when we talked.

Her problem wasn't "mental illness." It was fear and insecurity. She didn't fully understand who God is and that we can trust Him with anything and everything. Eventually, her faith grew and trust in Him developed. She began to leave off the foil and feel comfortable again. She came to church, engaged with people, and reunited with her husband.

Yes, I could have suggested a psych hospital for her. They would have treated her "condition" with medications and psychotherapy—none of which would have touched the core of her problem. At her core, she didn't know God.

As I wrote in *Counseling: How to Counsel Biblically*, "In my counseling experience I have had many people who exhibited bizarre behavior tell me later that they did so intentionally to get attention. In some cases, they have practiced this kind of behavior so often that it has become a habit pattern that is basically an unplanned, automatic, reflex reaction. It has become a way of life."[3] They get caught up in the game they're playing.

"The iniquities of the wicked ensnare him, and he is held fast in the cords of his sin" (Prov. 5:22).
"Put off your old self, which belongs to your former manner of life and is corrupt through deceitful desires" (Eph. 4:22).

People can change. We must not be daunted in our efforts to help them—even if their actions are bizarre.

Many times, people come to us with psychological or psychiatric diagnoses they have been labeled with—by themselves or by others. Schizophrenia, codependency, addiction, multiple personality disorder, borderline personality disorder, separation anxiety disorder, bipolar disorder, etc.

What do we do with this? These people are certainly tormented, but by what? We must ask ourselves if the cause of their behavior is first of all, organic or nonorganic in nature. The chart at the end of this chapter may be helpful.

If the problem is truly organic, then steps can be taken to treat it. Sometimes medications are necessary. Sometimes it involves helping the person resolve physical issues like sleep deprivation or eating or drinking harmful things (too much caffeine, wheat, salt or sugar, drugs or alcohol). Sometimes it involves encouraging the person to start exercising, which has been shown to be a terrific stress-reliever—especially when combined with spiritual meditations.

Before assuming the counselee's problems are nonorganic and launching headlong in the wrong direction, we should explore the causes more thoroughly. A doctor's visit should be scheduled. Tests should be run, including labs where this is appropriate. We should rule out any physical cause before we explore a non-physical one.

Sometimes the cause is both. For instance, someone could come to us with problems resulting from sleep deprivation. This is a physical problem. Yet, the reason for his sleep deprivation could be spiritual—like anxiety, worry, or lack of faith in God. We must consider and respond to both.

3   John MacArthur and The Master's College Faculty, *Counseling: How to Counsel Biblically*, Nelson Reference & Electronic, Nashville, TN, ©2005, pg. 154.

If the cause is nonorganic, we can then, through this process of *inventory* and *interpretation* (asking proper questions and properly interpreting the answers), determine the direction our biblical counseling must take. All this is necessary is we are to counsel effectively.

Possible Causes

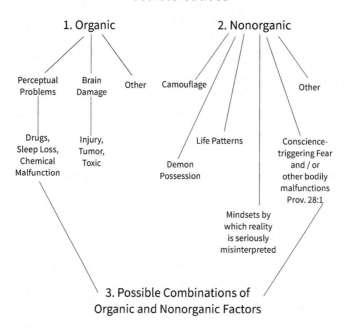

1. Organic   2. Nonorganic

Perceptual Problems   Brain Damage   Other   Camouflage   Other

Drugs, Sleep Loss, Chemical Malfunction   Injury, Tumor, Toxic   Life Patterns   Conscience-triggering Fear and / or other bodily malfunctions Prov. 28:1

Demon Possession

Mindsets by which reality is seriously misinterpreted

3. Possible Combinations of Organic and Nonorganic Factors

6

Instruction

A ah. Instruction! This is the area that most counselors are more familiar and comfortable with. In many cases, this is because they think this is the part of counseling where they can shine! They can preach the Word and, by doggies, that's what they want to do.

But hold on a sectond. I hate to burst your bubble, but that's not what instruction is all about. This is not the part where we preach sermons and rain judgment down from on high. Let's start from the beginning, shall we?

Remember, our goal here is not to impress anyone with our brilliance and our dynamic preaching abilities. The goal is still to help people change, through a biblical process. Helping people change is what biblical counseling is all about. It's not about us. It's about them.

When we get to heaven, we will have no more need for biblical counseling because there will be no more need for change. But here on earth, there will always be a need for counseling. As long as we're in this world, we will have a need for change. "For now we see in a mirror dimly, but then face to face. Now I know in part; then I shall know fully, even as I have been fully known" (1 Cor. 13:12).

True biblical change sometimes requires help. At times, biblical counseling and discipleship are the means God uses to effect that change. Being a loving parent means training your children in discipleship, as well. Even when counseling our friends and family, we could be the means God uses to produce change in others—and in ourselves. "But exhort one another every day, as long as it is called 'today,' that none of you may be hardened by the deceitfulness of sin" (Heb. 3:13).

Therefore, the *right kind of instruction* is necessary to true biblical change. In biblical counseling, we're not interested in mere behavior modification—which is rarely effective in the long term. We're interested in changing the core of the problem, and in providing tools to be used in the future. We want to help our counselees change internally as well as externally.

We must also have the *right reason* for wanting to help people change. It's not so they will become more productive people, or to make ourselves look good, or to assist in their leapfrogging over a tough time. No, the reason for wanting to help others is for the glory of God. In helping people change, our goal is, like God's, to bring them more into the likeness of Christ.

Paul states the main concern of biblical counseling in Colossians 1:28-29. "Him we proclaim, warning everyone and teaching everyone with all wisdom, that we may present everyone mature in Christ. For this I toil, struggling with all his energy that he powerfully works within me." Yes, it's hard work, but like Paul says, it is not of our strength but in the strength and energy He supplies.

How do we promote this kind of true biblical change? That's what this chapter is about. We've already discussed some of the key elements of biblical change—*Involvement, Inspiration, Inventory,* and *Interpretation.* I hope you've seen how interwoven these are in the relationships we build with our counselees, disciples, children, or brothers and sisters in Christ.

Now it's important to understand the role and nature of *Instruction.* As always, that includes the *why, what,* and *how* of the instruction effective biblical counselors should deliver.

To start off this discussion, let's take another case study.

His name is Jim. Here's the conversation.

"So, Jim, I hear you saying that you would like to meet with me because you're feeling depressed and want some help in overcoming that depression. Let's see what we can do about it."

"Good," responds the college sophomore, "I'm hoping to find some relief from this soon."

"First of all, Jim, do you know Jesus Christ as your personal Savior?"

"Yes, I do, Mr. Smith. I've been a Christian since I was a young child. I accepted Christ into my heart when my Sunday School teacher told us about heaven and hell. As she explained it, I knew I wanted to go to heaven and I knew I didn't want to go to hell. So when she urged us to pray a prayer to ask Jesus into our hearts, I did what she told us to do."

The counselor pauses before continuing. "So you've asked Jesus to come into your heart, and because of what you did then, you now know that you are a child of God and that He is your Father and that you have eternal life?"

"Yes, that's right."

"Well, then, as a child of God, it's important for you to know and meditate on the promises of God. How much Scripture do you know? Have you memorized any of it?"

"I guess I'm somewhat familiar with some Bible verses. When I was younger, I went to Awana Club at church where they emphasized the importance of memorizing Scripture. Every week we were given Scripture verses to memorize and when we got together, we would be asked to repeat them. So I did memorize some Scripture. However, after I got out of Awana, I gave up the practice of memorizing Scripture and, to be honest, I don't really remember a lot of the verses I memorized back then."

"Well, if you really want to get over your depression, you'd better get back into that practice. I think you're probably having a problem with depression because you just don't know enough Scripture. So, before we get together next time, I'm going to ask you to memorize several verses of Scripture. Memorizing these verses will help you get back on track and pull you out of this depression. I want you to memorize Philippians 4:4, Galatians 5:22-23, Luke 2:10, James 1:2, and John 16:24. Then, when you start getting depressed, I want you to remind yourself of these verses. I think they will help you understand that, as a Christian, you have much to be joyful about."

With this being the case, let's now review this dialogue and evaluate its effectiveness. What does this information indicate about the counselor's work in the area of *involvement*? How would you evaluate his efforts in fulfilling this important aspect of the counseling process? What about *inspiration*? How much hope did he inspire to young Jim? How would you evaluate the counselor's efforts in fulfilling this important aspect of the counseling process? Next, let's review his attempts at taking a thorough *inventory*. How did he do in this area? What does this counselor really know about Jim? What information was he lax in obtaining? How would you evaluate his efforts in fulfilling this important aspect of the counseling process?

How did he do with *interpretation*? Did he truly discern the biblical nature and causes of the counselee's problems? What does this case study indicate about the counselor's work in the area of interpretation? What conclusions did he reach about the nature and cause of Jim's depression? How would you evaluate the counselor's efforts in fulfilling this important aspect of the counseling process?

I think we would all agree that this counselor was woefully inefficient in each of these categories. So how did he embrace his responsibility to provide relevant, godly *instruction* for Jim? Again, he was woefully inefficient.

Let's consider what he should have done. To help people like Jim, biblical counselors should attempt to skillfully implement all of the elements of biblical change that we've discussed.

Yet, doing these things is not really enough to help poor Jim, or anyone else. Involvement is important, but it's not enough. Inspiration is vital but again, not enough. Inventory is greatly helpful, but it is not enough. Accurately interpreting the nature and cause of Jim's problems is important, but it is not enough.

If the counselor is going to be of maximum help, he must go beyond the first four key elements to this one. He must give Jim the *right kind of instruction* (counsel). After all, he's a counselor. He should counsel.

But what is the right kind of instruction an effective biblical counselor should offer to people like Jim? The answer is,

Instruction that is biblical in nature. It's not important what the counselor's personal opinions and thoughts are on the issue. What is important is what *God's* thoughts and teachings are on the issue. The counselor is to skillfully convey that to the one who has come to him for guidance and help.

Our instruction must possess three basic requirements:

- It must be biblically based;
- It must be biblically accurate;
- It must be biblically sound.

We don't base our counsel on the wisdom of the world, but upon the wisdom of the Word! We must not take a *Psychology Today* approach to instruction. Instead, an effective biblical counselor will make God and His truth the central part of his instruction. He will base all instructions on the teaching of His Word. Why?

- Because he believes the Bible is a practical book. It's a "lamp to my feet and a light to my path" (Ps. 119:105). (See also 2 Tim. 3:16–17, 2 Pet. 1:3–4.)
- Because he believes the Bible is the only resource for counseling that deals with all of the practical problems of life in an absolutely reliable and trustworthy fashion. (See Ps. 19:9, Ps. 119:89, 2 Tim. 3:16.)
- Because he believes the Bible provides whatever is true and necessary for successful living. It is completely adequate. (See 2 Peter 1:3, Isa. 8:19–20, John 17:17.)

In Jim's case, the counselor did say a few things that reflected biblical truth. For instance, he referred to Jesus as a "personal Savior." He emphasized the importance of faith in Christ, of the forgiveness of sins, of knowing the Bible. He asserted that Christians have reasons for rejoicing and that the Bible does have the solution to our problems. All that is true.

However, while the instruction Jim's counselor gave was somewhat biblical in nature, it was biblically deficient in terms of its appropriateness and adequacy. So, what did he do wrong? How was his instruction deficient?

First, it was too abstract and general

Though true, his instructions were not adequate or sufficient or specific enough to help Jim know the true nature and cause of his depression. His instruction did nothing to help Jim figure out what to do to overcome his depression. His only solution was to memorize Scripture. Let's get specific here. What things should the counselor have done that he just didn't do?

- Though Jim said Jesus was his personal Savior, the counselor has no idea what Jim meant by that term. He used the word *trust* but didn't investigate Jim's understanding of what that means.
- He never investigated why Jim was depressed, what led him to seek counsel, and how Jim's depression was manifesting in his life.
- He never investigated how long this depression had been going on.
- He never gathered the data the PREACHD acronym emphasized.
- He never tried to find out what was going on in Jim's heart.
- He never investigated Jim's support systems, or whether he was motivated by the love of the Father or the love of the world.

Next, he violated the directions of Proverbs 18:13

"If one gives an answer before he hears, it is his folly and shame." He never really understood the nature or the causes of Jim's depression. As a result, he gave him some good general biblical advice, but the instruction he gave was not as helpful or relevant as it would have been if he had first gathered the right kind of information, and made the right kind of interpretation. Only after doing this can a counselor know what specific instruction is needed.

The counselor could have made his instruction more helpful if he had conducted the session in the following way. First, he could have thanked Jim for coming in for help and maybe for filling out the PDI form he was given.

He could have said something like this. "Jim, I'm so glad you came here today because I'm convinced that if you're truly a Christian and willing to do what God wants you to do, there is absolute hope that you can overcome this depression. Help is available to you through God's Word. In deciding the best counsel I can offer you, I first need to thoroughly understand your situation, so I need to ask some questions. I hope you'll feel comfortable answering them. Is that okay with you?"

Next, a really important matter: you should go to the Lord in prayer at this point, asking God for guidance and wisdom in overcoming this issue. Prayer should be an important part of every counseling session.

Then it's helpful to explore Jim's situation a little more. Ask him questions about his college, about his interests, about his favorite and least favorite classes, about his friendships and his circumstances. Get to know him a bit. Help him relax by establishing this genuine involvement with him.

Next, explore spiritual issues. You might start with, "You have said that you're saved. What does being saved mean to you?" Then progress to some matters like these: "Tell me how you came to know Christ. Give me a description of your spiritual pilgrimage. What has happened in your life since you became a believer? What are some of your spiritual highs and lows? What kind of devotional practices do you engage in? Do you believe in the Bible as the inerrant Word of God? What about your church? How often do you attend? How involved are you? How are you being helped through your church involvement? How does God fit into your life right now? Would you like to know what God says about why people get depressed and what to do about it when it happens? Are you open to implementing the principles the Bible sets forth?"

About his depression, it's important to know how he perceives it. You'll want to find out what he means by "depression." When did it start? What steps has he already tried to help with this problem? What was the most helpful thing so far? How has his depression affected his life? What about his sleep habits? Eating? Exercise? Relationships?

Find out what he thinks his greatest strengths and weaknesses are. What brings him the greatest joy? What brings him the greatest sorrow?

Ask him if he ever thinks that perhaps God is letting him down, that He has forgotten him, or that he's not getting a fair shake from God. Find out if he's angry with God or brokenhearted and feeling betrayed or abandoned.

Does he ever feel he's been given more than he can bear, that it's too much for him to handle? Does he believe his problems are unsolvable?

You see how asking these types of questions gets into the heart of the issues surrounding Jim? By delving into these specific issues, an effective biblical counselor begins to truly comprehend who Jim is and the nature and causes of his problems. He demonstrates to Jim that he cares about him and can point him to appropriate answers to his specific concerns.

Show him that there is a difference between the lies the enemy (Satan) tells us and the truth found in God's Word.

Lies vs. Truths

THE ENEMY'S LIES	GOD'S TRUTH FOUND IN HIS WORD
Because of what has been done to me, I am a . . . . Because I came from a dysfunctional family, I am not responsible for my behavior, feelings, thoughts, attitudes, and reactions.	My circumstances (past and present) do have an influence on me, but I am not helpless. I am fully responsible.
I do what I do and feel as I feel and think as I do because I am a needy person and my needs are not being met.	I do what I do and feel and think as I do because I am a sinner; I behave the way I do because I am selfish; I want something and I'm not getting it or I'm getting something I don't want. I worship and serve my own desires; I am more concerned about pleasing myself than I am about pleasing and worshiping God. I worship and serve myself rather than the God of the Bible.

The Enemy's Lies	God's Truth Found in His Word
My problems are bigger and more difficult than the problems of other people. I'm in a different category from most people.	My trials and difficulties are not unique. They are common to man. I am not in a category all by myself.
God has forgotten me. If God really cared, He wouldn't allow these things to happen to me; He wouldn't allow people to treat me the way they do. He wouldn't allow the bad things that I experience to happen.	God is faithful; God is good; God is my ever-present help in the time of trouble. I will never be separated from the love of God (Ps. 34:10; 46:1; Rom. 8:32–39).
I can't handle what God has allowed to come into my life. It's more than I can bear. I simply can't take it any longer.	God will not give me more than I can bear. He knows my load limit. He won't make the furnace hotter than I can stand nor keep me in it longer than I can take.
I'm trapped. There's no way out. It's hopeless. It's meaningless. No good can come out of this.	God will always provide a way of escape. There is a way out. God is up to something, and it will ultimately be something good. My trials and difficulties do have meaning and purpose.
I behave in the unbiblical way I do because my love tank has not been filled, because others have failed to love, appreciate, esteem, respect, and treat me the way I should have been treated. I lack the security that comes from knowing that others love me; that comes from knowing I really belong.	I behave in unbiblical ways because I am selfish, I worship myself, I am an idolater, and I love myself more than I love God and others.
I behave in unbiblical ways because I lack self-esteem, have a bad self-image, hate myself, and I lack self-respect.	I behave in unbiblical ways because I am too self-focused; I love myself too much and I don't have enough Christ-esteem; I am not willing to lose my life for the sake of Christ and others.

THE ENEMY'S LIES	GOD'S TRUTH FOUND IN HIS WORD
I behave in unbiblical ways because I don't feel good about myself, because I'm not happy; I am not making the impact that I would like to make, because I and others don't think I'm very significant. I mean, I'm not as talented or as intelligent as other people; I can't do what they do and I don't have the opportunities they have.	I behave in unbiblical ways for the reasons that were mentioned in the previous statements under the "God's Truth" column. I behave in unbiblical ways because I am proud and dissatisfied with the abilities God has given me; I am not taking advantage of the opportunities God has given me. I am jealous of the gifts and opportunites of others. My main goal in life is to glorify myself rather than God; I am too concerned about me.

"The Enemy's Lies" are wrong because they put the major emphasis on deprivation, whereas the Bible puts the emphasis on depravity. They are wrong because none of them can be supported by Scripture—truth. They are wrong because they contradict the Bible's explanation of why we behave and feel and think badly.

According to the Bible, the main reason we have problems is because we love, fear, trust, serve, and listen to idols which come to us in the form of our own desires for prestige, self-glorification, self-esteem, control, power, popularity, approval, respect, pleasure, possessions, success, good feelings, etc., rather than worshiping, loving, fearing, trusting, listening to, wanting to please, obey, and glorify God.

Let's take another look at the main lies described in 1 Corinthians 10:13 and contrast those main lies with the truth of God's Word. "No temptation has overtaken you that is not common to man. God is faithful, and he will not let you be tempted beyond your ability, but with the temptation he will also provide the way of escape, that you may be able to endure it."

THE ENEMY SAYS:

- Your problems are unique, bigger, and tougher than other people's.
- God has forgotten you.
- Your problems are more than you can bear.
- You are trapped, and there is no way out.
- You are all alone in the world. Nobody cares.

GOD'S TRUTH SAYS:

- You are dealing with common temptations.
- I am faithful.
- I will not let you be tempted beyond what you can bear.
- I will provide a way out so that you can stand up under it.
- I will always love you.

You see, if Jim's counselor had taken this approach and asked questions such as these, he would have gleaned information that would have guided him to give Jim the kind of instruction that was not only biblical in content, but also appropriately, adequately, and specifically biblical. It would have been truly helpful if he had been able to use Scripture that was more relevant to Jim and his issues.

Our job as biblical counselors is to be a bridge on which the truth of God is delivered to people in a relevant, appropriate, and specific way.

God's Accurate and Appropriate Truth  The Counselee and His Problems

It is not enough for us to use a *shotgun* approach. We are not to deliver general biblical truth in abstract, nonspecific ways and hope it hits someone. We must use a *rifle* approach. We are to deliver the truth of God with specificity and clarity and relevance.

What are the characteristics of appropriate and relevant

biblical instruction? We must counsel people in such a way that it is specific to their particular situation or problem. Generalities are not often helpful. And the more we understand people, the better we can design instruction that is specific to their needs.

What category is your counselee in right now? What is his greatest need? What does he need to hear first? Is his need of the moment for:

- Reproof, correction, and/or training? (See 2 Tim. 3:15–17.)
- Entreaty? Begged on behalf of Christ? (See 2 Cor. 5:20–21.)
- Gentle correction? (See 2 Tim. 2:24–26.)
- Exhortation, rebuke? (See Titus 2:15.)
- Instruction, information, reminders, encouragement and comfort? (See 1 Thess. 4:13.)
- Praise, commendation? Or patient instruction and teaching? Or to be admonished/encouraged? (See 1 Thess. 5:11–14.)

Once we know what our counselee needs, we need to gear our instruction to his level of spiritual maturity. A huge range exists between babies in Christ and mature believers.

Babies lack the ability to handle solid food, are extremely "feeling" oriented, lack self-control, are self-centered, tend to hero worship, and are easily impressed and led astray. Mature believers, however, can handle strong teaching, are concerned about others, are not impressed with externals, not easily led astray, esteem others better than themselves, are peacemakers, have a lifestyle that is distinctly different from unsaved people, appreciate all of God's true servants, and aren't hero-worshippers.

We must tailor our counsel to our counselee's level of maturity. We must also tailor our counsel to his emotional condition. Is he a bruised reed, as Matthew 12:20 says? He needs to be handled gently. Sometimes we weep with those who weep. Like Proverbs 25:20 says, we should not sing frivolous songs to a person with a troubled heart. We must be sensitive to what this hurting one is experiencing.

We must also tailor our instruction to his receptivity. We don't cast our pearls before swine (Matt. 7:6). We don't answer a fool according to his folly (Prov. 26:4–5). Matthew 10:13–14 tells us if we go into a house and the people there receive us and our words, we are to stay. If they don't, we are to leave.

Lastly, we must tailor our teaching and instruction to the counselee's learning style. No one method of instruction fits all people. We all have ways we learn best. Some are auditory learners, some need to see it written down, some need to perform a function, and some need to write it all out. Jesus approached Nicodemus and the Samarian woman very differently. He customized His teaching. Therefore, we must adapt to the method our counselee learns best. Here are some questions we must answer. Do we . . .

- Woo or caution?
- Issue promises or warnings?
- Provide direct or indirect instruction?
- Provide books, recordings, or videos?
- Use prepared studies or freelance?
- Use the counselee's own example or the example of others?
- Use role play or discussion?
- Provide detailed instructions or general instructions?
- Give large amounts of homework or small amounts?
- Give memory work or not?

Other considerations include these points:

- Are we encouraging or convicting?
- What analogies or illustrations will be most effective?
- What research projects might be effective?

The list goes on. The point is that we can't answer any of those questions if we don't get to know our counselees. We must get to know what the real issues are in the lives of people.

This next point should go without saying, but I'll mention it anyway. We must know the Scriptures if we are to be effective biblical counselors. A craftsman must have a good, working knowledge of each tool in his toolbox. He needs to not only know what the tool is but how to use it best. So should we. (See Matt. 22:29, 2 Tim. 2:15, Ps. 1:2, Ps. 119:9–11.)

We are to know our tools—the Scriptures. And we must know how to rightly interpret God's Word.

When effective biblical counselors give biblical instruction, they must make sure they understand and explain the meaning of important Bible words in accordance with what they meant to the writers and original recipients of Scripture. These are words like hope, joy, justification, love, repentance, regeneration, sanctification, fornication, adultery, grace, submission, sensuality, wisdom, hypocrisy, legalism, and humility. The list goes on. If we are to convey their meaning appropriately, we must understand their meaning well.

Not only must we comprehend the meaning of key words, but we must also be able to explain passages in keeping with the immediate and larger context in which these passages are found. Many erroneous interpretations occur because people interpret passages without paying attention to their context.

We must also have understanding of the purposes for which these passages were intended. The Bible is filled with verses which explain the Holy Spirit's purposes for giving the Word to us. (See passages like 2 Tim. 3:15-17, 2 Peter 1:3-4, Ps. 19:7-11, Ps. 119:4, 11, 38, 50, 52, 66, 105.)

The concept of "putting off" and "putting on" is frequently addressed in the New Testament. We must do an effective job of teaching this concept to those who come to us for help. The following charts may help in this endeavor.

PUT OFF	PUT ON
Self-oriented way of life	God-oriented way of life
Broad way that leds to death	Narrow way that leads to life
Inordinate selfish desires	Pleasing God and serving others' desires
Fear of man	Fear of the Lord
Idolatry	Worship of God alone
Being ruled by felt needs	Renewed mind; being ruled by God's Word
Deep yearnings, cravings	Heavenlymindedness
Autonomy from God	Dependence on God
Selfish goals/expectations	Desires of the Spirit
False hopes/trusts	Confidence in God and His promises
Pride, arrogance, haughtiness	Humility, lowliness of mind
Self-righteousness	Acceptance of Christ's righteousness
Malice	Kindness, goodness
Self-esteem, admiration	Christ-esteem, esteem of others
Honoring self	Honoring others first
Feeling-orientation, sensuality	Principle-drivenness
Anger, hostility, bitterness	Love, self-control, forgiveness, mercy
Negativity, discontentment	Gratitude, contentment
Defensiveness, blame-shifting	Acceptance of criticism
Self-justification, unrepentant spirit	Repentance, confession of sin
Impatience, annoyance, irritability	Patience, gentleness, calmness, forbearance
Factiousness, argumentativeness, critical spirit	Being a peacemaker, being hospitable, showing appreciation
Unwholesome, destructive speech	Wholesome, edifying, constructive speech
Laziness, slothfulness	Diligence, industriousness
Etc.	Etc.

I've given you a lot to think about in the area of instruction. Now it's time to consider the next element we'll discuss—*Inducement*. What in the world is that?

7

Inducement

Inducement means, "to influence to act; to prevail upon; to motivate; to provide incentive; to lead a person to a conclusion by some particular path or course of reasoning."[4] Inducement, as I apply it to the biblical counseling process, means "to describe an aspect of counseling in which the counselor attempts to persuade, motivate and/or influence the counselee to make certain commitments or decisions that will facilitate true biblical change."

This chapter will explain the *why, what* and *how* of Inducement. In the *why,* I hope to demonstrate the key role counselee commitment plays in the process of true biblical change. The *what* clarifies the various kinds of commitments that facilitate true biblical change. In the *how,* I want to present biblical ways of motivating or persuading or inducing people to make the important commitments that promote actual biblical change.

Why is Inducement an important aspect of the process of true biblical change?

Because the Bible emphasizes the crucial role inducement (commitment) plays in the process of change.

Here are a few of many passages I could use to support this assertion:

• "Then Moses stood in the gate of the camp and said, 'Who

is on the LORD's side? Come to me.' And all the sons of Levi gathered around him" (Ex. 32:26).

- "I have made a covenant with my eyes; how then could I gaze at a virgin?" (Job 31:1).
- "I appeal to you therefore, brothers, by the mercies of God, to present your bodies as a living sacrifice, holy and acceptable to God, which is your spiritual worship" (Rom. 12:1).
- "Therefore, knowing the fear of the Lord, we persuade others. But what we are is known to God, and I hope it is known also to your conscience" (2 Cor. 5:11).
- "I therefore, a prisoner for the Lord, urge you to walk in a manner worthy of the calling to which you have been called" (Eph. 4:1).

Each of these verses is talking about commitment—either making one or urging others to make one. I can't tell you how important both of these actions are to the biblical counseling process. Other effective biblical counselors will affirm this.

Therefore, the Bible, as well as counseling experience, emphasizes and illustrates the importance of inducing or motivating people to make a commitment if real change is to take place. People usually don't change by chance—but by choice. Because of that, effective biblical counselors must be involved in inducing (motivating) people to make a commitment to change.

Don't confuse this with manipulation. A real distinction separates manipulation from motivation. Manipulation almost always involves inducing a change for the manipulator's benefit. Motivation almost always involves inducing a change for the good of the other person—especially when that change correlates to the clear teaching of Scripture.

As well as a difference in meaning and ultimate benefit, there is a difference in methods. For instance, in a police interrogation, the concept of good cop / bad cop exists. Think of a situation where police personnel make promises they never intend to keep in order to obtain a confession from a criminal. This would be considered manipulation.

The method involved in biblical counseling is quite different. This includes practicing all the elements I've already discussed to the end that *inducement* may be applied after a genuine relationship has developed. And that ultimate end points the counselee to Christ and supports commitments for him to follow Christ in obedience. This is always for the other person's benefit, not for ours.

What kinds of commitments should we seek for those we're trying to help?

The first is the commitment to make the Bible the counselee's final authority. If he does not view the Bible as such, biblical counseling will not be helpful to him. The passages we hold out to him will be meaningless and unproductive unless he views the Bible as God's authoritative, inerrant, relevant, perfect Word. This would be, in essence, casting pearls before swine. So this must be a prerequisite for a successful biblical counseling relationship. (See Isa. 8:19-20, Ps. 119:128, John 17:17, 2 Tim. 3:15–17.)

Another important commitment is to trust and depend on Christ (not on self or on others) for grace and the resources needed to make the changes God wants him to make. So many passages in the Bible attest to this. (See James 4:6–10, Ps. 147:6, Luke 18:9–14, 1 Thess. 1:9, Isa. 30:15, Jude 24–25, Ps. 20:7, 2 Cor. 9:8, and Isa. 26:3–4, to name a few.)

It's helpful for both the counselor and the counselee to call all that is unbiblical by the biblical names God calls them. For instance, a weakness is sin, a one-night stand is fornication or adultery, a same-sex attraction is immorality or homosexuality (See 1 John 3:4, 1 John 1:9, Ps. 51:1–3.)

Another helpful commitment is to accept personal responsibility for all unbiblical motives, thoughts, actions, and feelings. Blame-shifting is not helpful. (See Ps. 32, Rom. 3:19, Rom. 14:10, Prov. 14:9.)

Excuses are unhelpful in the biblical counseling setting, as well. We often hear people excuse their sins or shortcomings with phrases like these:

- I can't.
- If he hadn't done that, I wouldn't have done this.

- I've tried that and it didn't work.
- I don't have time to do it.
- I'm one of those people who is highly strung, a worrywart, etc.
- That's just the way I am.
- If you were in my place, you'd. . . .
- You just don't understand how badly I've been treated.

These statements must not go unchallenged. Take note of them while listening so you can come back to them later. Then gently move your counselee past these excuses as he commits to accept responsibility for his actions.

Here is a big one! So many people are "feeling" oriented. Yes, we understand what they're feeling, but an effective biblical counselor moves them beyond what they're feeling to what God expects of them. They must commit to persevere in doing what God wants them to do regardless of how they feel. (See Gen. 22:1ff, Matt. 26:36–46, Heb 12:1–4.)

What kinds of things should biblical counselors do to induce or motivate people to make the necessary commitments required for true biblical change to occur?

I believe we need three types of skill to induce commitment. The first is skill in identifying the presence of resistance in the counselee. They may demonstrate their resistance in two primary ways.

1. Overt (Mark 10:17–26, Matt. 21:28–32). These will tell you plainly they do not want to participate or engage or be open and honest. They may even tell you they see no purpose in biblical counseling.
2. Covert, Subtle (Luke 6:46, Matt. 21:28–32). These won't tell you directly but will demonstrate their resistance in passive ways, such as the following:

a. Cancellations;
b. Homework failure;
c. Repeated tardiness;
d. Distancing, lack of openness;
e. Threats, intimidation;
f. Manipulation;
g. Sidetracking;
h. Argumentativeness, negativism;
i. Blame-shifting, excuse-making;
j. Storytelling, rambling to deflect the issue.

A second needed skill is the ability to discern the reasons for such resistance—and I've heard many. It's important to figure out why the resistance is present—why the counselee's compliance is absent. This could be due to:

- Lack of salvation;
- Lack of desire or inclination;
- Ignorance;
- Discouragement;
- Fear;
- Pride;
- Bad theology or bad teaching;
- Doubts;
- Bitterness, resentment, desire for revenge;
- Enjoying the pleasures of sin—not truly wanting to turn from them;
- Victim mentality;
- Misunderstanding the role of feelings in the Christian life
- Black-and-white sin mentality;
- Laziness, slothfulness.

The third skill is having the ability to persuade and motivate. Some actually lack skill in counteracting and overcoming this kind of resistance to biblical counsel. If this is the case, I'm awfully thankful you're holding this book in your hands right now. Skills can be taught. That's the goal of this book.

Perhaps your problem with this is ignorance or inexperience

in counseling. Perhaps you're discouraged and you need godly encouragement. Perhaps you're afraid to confront, challenge, to hold someone else accountable, or to question motives for resistance. No matter what the obstacle to obtaining this skill, I believe these eight "I"s will help you develop what is lacking. Allow me to offer some suggestions.

Once resistance is detected, we must carefully explain and clarify what the Bible says about it, his situation, his responses, his desires and the goals he says are important to him. We should assure them the Bible has the way to solve his problems.

Remember to adapt your confrontation style to the personality and tendencies of your counselee. Play back actual words, phrases, or behaviors if needed to support your assertion that he is resisting in some way. Welcome feedback, questions, disagreements, explanations or perspectives. Allow for the possibility you could be wrong about his resistance.

What are some models of godly methods of inducement?

How about an example using God, Himself? His relationship with Moses met with a great deal of resistance, didn't it? Let's outline the steps in the flow of that "counseling session."

- God commanded Moses (Ex. 3:10).
- Moses expresses resistance (Ex. 3:11).
- God practiced inducement Ex. (3:12).
- Moses continued to resist (Ex. 3:13).
- God practices inducement (Ex. 3:14–22).
- Moses continues to resist (Ex. 4:1).
- God practiced inducement (Ex. 4:11).
- Moses continued to resist (Ex. 4:13).
- God practiced inducement (Ex. 4:14–18).
- Moses stopped resisting and decided to obey (Ex. 4:18–20).

What a great example for us. Let's look at some of the features of God's inducement process. First of all, God took the concerns of Moses seriously, and showed respect and concern for him.

Moses had some legitimate concerns about what God was asking him to do—he felt fear and had a sense of inadequacy, unbelief, discouragement over past failures, and tranquility in his present lifestyle.

God listened. Then He addressed and overcame the reasons for resistance. He used godly promises. He gave concrete, attainable goals and assured Moses of success. He declared exactly who and what He was. He outlined specific instructions about what He wanted Moses to do. He gave Moses a demonstration of His power. He asked probing, thought-provoking questions and skillfully showed the perspectives Moses was overlooking.

When Moses kept resisting, He was gentle but persistent. He assured Moses that He would be with him, that He would give him the power to do what He was commanding him to do. Repeatedly, He gave Moses reassurance that he would be successful if he obeyed Him. He reminded him that his success was not dependent on his own power, wisdom and skill, but on the wisdom and power of the living God. Even though He expressed His displeasure with Moses' continued resistance, He was kind when reassuring him of His continued presence with him.

What lessons can we learn from this example? Here are a few. To promote commitment in another person, you must:

- Properly identify the reasons for resistance;
- Respond with appropriate biblical antidotes to these reasons;
- Not be surprised if people continue to struggle with obedience to God's directives. Moses is presented as one of the godliest men in the Bible and yet he struggled with this.
- Be patient, slow to anger, slow to give up on a person when he doesn't immediately respond in a positive way to inducement. Be willing to repeat and expand on what you have previously stated. Look on the resistant behavior as an opportunity to bring God and His promises into clearer focus—as a teaching opportunity.

The writer of Hebrews gave us a New Testament example to follow. Read Hebrews. Repeatedly, he instructed, encouraged, and exhorted. He reminded his readers of the blessing they have in Christ. He rebuked them for their neglect and failure. He expressed his personal concern and desire for them to obey, reminding them of the goodness, greatness, compassion and faithfulness of God. He continued to teach and commend and encourage. He gave great examples of the faithful believers from the past. He warned and encouraged them about God's hand of discipline for disobedience, but still spoke about the compassion of Christ for them, encouraging them, reminding them of God's promises. The book of Hebrews is an amazing example of inducement.

If you'd like to see some lessons learned from this masterful account in Hebrews, review the ones already listed from the Old Testament. They're the same.

What do we do if we cannot overcome all the resistance we find?

It would be nice if everyone you counsel would, without any resistance, commit to the important truths you ask them to. However, this is the real world. And in our real world that is not always the case. Do you give up on them? Do you throw a temper tantrum and order them out of your office? I don't think so.

So, what do you do? I have some suggestions for you. These are still biblically consistent even though they may not be your first choice in helping your counselee.

1. An effective biblical counselor may choose to temporarily offer a lesser, partial commitment for a few sessions. See if your counselee's resistance begins to fade as your relationship with him continues to develop.
2. An effective biblical counselor may choose to enlist the help of significant others. This is not always ideal, but for certain cases, it can prove helpful.
3. An effective biblical counselor may find it helpful to have the counselee write out a commitment statement and then have him sign it.
4. An effective biblical counselor may find it helpful to have the counselee fill out and sign a commitment to change cove-

nant making himself accountable to someone else. Here's one example of this:

Commitment to Change Covenant

• •

Desiring with all my heart to please God and to be a better ___, I purpose with the certain help of God, my Savior, I will

- Admit it when I am wrong and. . . .
- Keep the house clean and. . . .
- Have devotions routinely.
- Do the fix-it jobs. . . .
- Express appreciation. . . .
- Spend thirty minutes a day doing. . . .
- Plan a daily schedule. . . .
- Do at least two fun things. . . .

Signed _____
Witnessed _____
Date _____

5. An effective biblical counselor may have to implement the third and fourth steps of church discipline, described in Matthew 18:15–17. It rarely comes to this, but if the counselee's resistance prevents his adhering to the Word of God, it may be necessary. Each case must be considered with great soberness.

I don't mean to end this important chapter on this negative note. Sometimes, even when church discipline is brought to bear, God grants repentance and draws the counselee back into a right relationship with Him and with the church. Such repentance is an inspiring, God-glorifying experience to witness.

True biblical change is entirely possible—even in difficult cases. We've already come a long way in examining the process for this biblical change. We began with *Involvement*, then progressed to *Inspiration, Inventory, Interpretation, Instruction* and now *Inducement*. The next step is no less important—*Implementation*.

8

Implementation

In this chapter, I hope to demonstrate the importance of this next step, *Implementation*, in the process of true biblical change. We also need to note the essential components of implementation. What is involved in promoting implementation in the biblical counseling setting? This chapter will provide some specific strategies to incorporate this step in your counseling relationships.

Why does an effective biblical counselor
need to focus on helping people implement
biblical principles into their lives?
Why is this step so important?

The first six "I"s are important. Don't get me wrong. But without this one, the others are ineffective in promoting true biblical change in people.

Our churches are filled with people who have heard that they should change their sinful practices. They know why they should change. They have been told why they have problems, and have been made aware that what they are doing and thinking may be wrong. They probably recognize that sin causes them to have "a bad heart." Yet, pastors and teachers are quick to point out that there is hope—that they can actually change, that God's Word holds promises that will guide them away from their sin.

Still, many of them either refuse to do what they know they should do, or they don't understand how to do it. They don't change. They still don't obey God's Word. They need help sometimes in knowing how to actually put God's Word into practice in their lives and painful situations.

That's where an effective biblical counselor comes in. We teach our counselees how to implement these principles and promises into their world in real, practical ways.

Many will never come to a counselor for that. They are content to sit in church, week after week, without exploring the very things that could help them. Why does this happen?

For one thing, they may not be believers at all. Some people attend church for unspiritual reasons. I know some single people who only go to church to find a spouse. I knew one man who came to church to network with the wealthier members so they'd do business with him. We can't assume that all church attendees are there for spiritual reasons.

For another thing, they may not be really committed to change. Even when they say they want to change, to live godlier lives in Christ, they may not actually mean it. If you really mean it, you put forth effort to do so.

Another reason they don't change may be due to ignorance. They may not know that help, in the form of biblical counseling, is available to them. Or they may think that their problems aren't serious enough to justify going to a biblical counselor.

Sadly, some believe their situation is hopeless, that they will never be able to change, and that they must merely "make the best of a bad situation." They keep their problems to themselves and, in doing so, rarely move forward with true biblical change.

Some don't believe they need anyone to help them. They believe they can change on their own, in their own power and wisdom. They think in terms of the power of the flesh rather than the power of the Spirit.

Often, people are just baffled about this whole process of biblical change. They may need help and training to be able to implement biblical truth into their lives and their situations. They're confused, so change doesn't happen.

What I wish to do in this chapter is to cover the "how to." In my book, *Fear Factor,* I spoke about having a proper fear of the Lord. When we begin to think too highly of ourselves, we think too lowly of God. In that book, I wrote,

> If the fear of God is as important for Christians as we have indicated, we would expect that God would not only give us information about the why and what of this issue, but also the how. And indeed, He has! We're going to see that God has a great deal to say about this aspect of developing, increasing and sustaining the fear of God in our lives.[5]

If we have the proper view of God and of His Word, we will find hope that change is possible. When we have a proper sense of who God is and what He can do, we begin to understand that the reason change is possible is because we serve a good God with unlimited power. He equips us to follow Him. He equips us to obey. "For it is God who works in you, both to will and to work for his good pleasure" (Phil. 2:13).

Scripture makes it crystal clear that God isn't satisfied for us to merely know the truth. He wants us to practice, obey, and implement the truth in our daily lives.

Here are just a few of the many verses I could have used to support this important truth.

- "But he said, 'Blessed rather are those who hear the word of God and keep it!'" (Luke 11:28).
- "What you have learned and received and heard and seen in me—practice these things, and the God of peace will be with you" (Phil. 4:9).
- "But be doers of the word, and not hearers only" (James 1:22).
- "So whoever knows the right thing to do and fails to do it, for him it is sin" (James 4:17).
- "And by this we know that we have come to know him, if we keep his commandments. Whoever says 'I know him' but does not keep his commandments is a liar, and the truth is not in him, but whoever keeps his word, in him truly the

5 Wayne and Joshua Mack, *The Fear Factor: What Satan Doesn't Want You to Know,* Hensley Publishing, Tulsa, Oklahoma, ©2002, p. 191.

love of God is perfected" (1 John 2:3-5).

- "Whoever keeps his commandments abides in him, and he in them" (1 John 3:24).

Since God's purpose is actualizing biblical truth in life, effective biblical counselors must do all they can to promote the implementation of this truth. The question is, what are the essential components that must be in place for implementation of biblical truth to occur?

One of the primary factors involved in helping people implement biblical truth is knowledge. We are to understand and have a knowledge of God's Word. (See John 17:17, Acts 20:32, Col. 2:1-5.) We are to possess a knowledge of God Himself. (See Dan. 11:32, 2 Peter 1:2-11, Phil. 3:10.) We must know God's promises, power, and purposes. (See 2 Peter 1:4, Rom. 15:4.) We are to comprehend His standards, precepts, and commands. (See Ps. 19:7-11, Ps. 119:105.) And we are to learn about ourselves through His Word—of our hearts, our sinful propensities, our weaknesses, and our strengths. (See Rom. 12:2-3, Phil. 3:12-14, Rom. 7:24.)

Perhaps the most essential factor for promoting the implementation of biblical truth is prayer. It has been said that Jesus never taught his disciples how to preach, but He did teach them how to pray.

Acts 4:31 says, "And when they had prayed, the place in which they were gathered together was shaken, and they were all filled with the Holy Spirit and continued to speak the word of God with boldness." Acts 6:4 supports this when it says, "But we will devote ourselves to prayer and to the ministry of the word." The disciples knew the importance of both—prayer and preaching the Word. They knew that if the ministry of the Word was to be successful, it must be preceded and followed by prayer.

Colossians 4:2-3 directs us to devote ourselves to prayer, praying that God may open a door for the Word. Paul stressed prayer in all of his letters, such as 2 Thessalonians 3:1 where he asks the brethren to pray for them, that the Word of the Lord may spread rapidly and be glorified. (See also examples in Acts 16:12-13, Eph. 6:18-19, Ezra 10:1.) I could go on and on.

In his book, *Spiritual Disciplines for the Christian Life,* Donald

Whitney has written this about prayer.

> God has not only spoken clearly and powerfully to us through Christ and the Scriptures. He also has a Very Large Ear continuously open to us. . . . Of all the Spiritual Disciplines, prayer is second only to the intake of God's Word in importance . . . one of the main reasons for a lack of Godliness is prayerlessness.[6]

In our book, *Life in the Father's House,* Dave Swavely and I exposited several biblical passages on prayer. Then we wrote that it is our firm conviction that

> the greatest need of our churches today is not for profound theologians or powerful preachers or other resources, though they are necessary and helpful. The greatest need is for people who will *pray* biblically, unceasingly and powerfully. . . . A church may not have the next Spurgeon in its pulpit and it may lack many resources for ministry, but if its people pray, it will be effective. . . . The spiritual battles for the souls of men, women, and children are not won when the preacher comes into the pulpit or the evangelist hits the streets. They are won before the preaching or evangelism [or counseling] even starts, by the people who come before the throne of God in prayer.[7]

Almost everyone would agree that the apostle Paul was one of the greatest and most widely used servants of God who ever lived. Wherever Paul went, he was used to bring people to Christ, to establish churches, and to help Christians put off sinful behaviors and thought patterns. Some of that was accomplished through his preaching and personal counseling. But I am convinced that if we could ask Paul to tell us why he was so effective, he would say that one of the greatest reasons

---

6   Donald S. Whitney, *Spiritual Disciplines for the Christian Life,* Navpress, Colorado Springs, CO, ©1991, p. 61–62.

7   Wayne A. Mack and David Swavely, *Life in the Father's House: A Member's Guide to the Local Church,* P&R Publishing, Phillipsburg, New Jersey, ©1996, p. 190.

was the prayers of the saints. Having people pray for a ministry or a body of Christ or even for individuals is the most effective activity we can do. It is only through the power of God that anything good can occur.

The final factor we'll discuss for promoting the implementation of biblical truth is planning. The well-known saying, "those who fail to plan, plan to fail" is supported by many passages of Scripture. Of the many I could quote, here are a few:

- "Commit your work to the LORD, and your plans will be established" (Prov. 16:3).
- "Everyone then who hears these words of mine and does them will be like a wise man who built his house on the rock. And the rain fell, and the floods came, and the winds blew and beat on that house, but it did not fall, because it had been founded on the rock. And everyone who hears these words of mine and does not do them will be like a foolish man who built his house on the sand. And the rain fell, and the floods came, and the winds blew and beat against that house, and it fell, and great was the fall of it" (Matt. 7:24–27).
- "Repay no one evil for evil, but give thought to do what is honorable in the sight of all" (Rom. 12:17).
- "This is why I left you in Crete, so that you might put what remained into order, and appoint elders in every town as I directed you" (Titus 1:5).
- "Come now, you who say, 'Today or tomorrow we will go into such and such a town and spend a year there and trade and make a profit'—yet you do not know what tomorrow will bring. What is your life? For you are a mist that appears for a little time and then vanishes. Instead you ought to say, 'If the Lord wills, we will live and do this or that'" (James 4:13–15).

These verses, and many more, emphasize the value of making a plan and following it. God wants us to be planners—planners dependent upon Him.

This is certainly true in the area of implementing biblical truth into our lives. People who succeed as Christians are people who make plans, asking for God's blessing upon them, eager and willing to change them if He shows them otherwise, and follow through till completion. Proverbs 21:5 says, "The plans of the diligent lead surely to abundance, but everyone who is hasty comes only to poverty."

In the biblical counseling arena, this is quite important. To do effective counseling or discipling, you must know how to plan and how to help others do it.

In what areas are you to plan in biblical counseling? First, an effective biblical counselor should plan (identify, think about) what God wants to accomplish in each situation. What goals should be present in counseling in general, and for each individual session?

Next, you should plan the issues you want to deal with in each specific case.

Third, you should plan the order in which you will deal with these issues. You must think about timing, approach, and effectiveness.

Then you should plan how you will deal specifically with these various issues. What methods and strategies will you use? Not only are you to consider each of these plans, but also plan what homework to assign. This takes much thought and consideration. In other words, it takes *planning* to know the most effective homework to assign in any given session.

Why is good homework so important?

- Good homework is beneficial in that it sets the pattern for action and change.
- Good homework clarifies expectations.
- Good homework promotes hope by communicating the idea that something can be done about the person's problems.
- Good homework puts the responsibility for change where it belongs.
- Good homework decreases the potential for dependence on the counselor.
- Good homework allows for gathering further data (from the homework itself as well as from the way the counselee does the homework).

- Good homework sustains the momentum between sessions.
- Good homework saves time—it shortens the length of the counseling period.
- Good homework provides a good starting point for each session.
- Good homework facilitates the implementation and practice of biblical principles essential to the development of godly habits.
- Good homework gives the counselee the tools he needs for future conflicts.
- The main benefit of good homework is this: The "golden hour" of counseling does not take place during the counseling session. It takes place, through the grace of the Holy Spirit, when the counselee spends time alone with God's Word. Giving good homework provides that time.

So, what constitutes "good homework"? It doesn't necessarily mean merely giving formal Bible studies for counselees to complete. It could also include filling in inventory/data sheets, writing journal entries, or keeping logs that may uncover unbiblical behaviors, responses, thoughts, or desires. It could include reading books, memorizing verses, listening to podcasts, doing daily devotionals, or watching sermons. You must be creative and make the homework worthwhile or your counselee may not be willing to keep doing it. (At the end of this chapter, I've included an extended list of the books I use most often. Yes, most of them are my own, but I wrote them for specific purposes, so I find them most useful.)

In designing good homework appropriate to your counselees, you may find yourself assigning extrabiblical activities. For instance, if the person is a couch potato, you may suggest physical exercise. Exercise is terrific for people with depression. If your counselee stays up late every night watching TV, you may ask him to try to go to bed at a reasonable hour and document how it feels to get a full night's sleep.

The "good homework" you assign may include the following types of activities:

- Physical
- Social
- Spiritual
- Recreational
- Occupational/scholastic
- Educational
- Interviews, visits
- Projects

Good homework is always appropriate to the person, to the problem, and to his present state of mind or condition. It needs to be specific and practical—always geared to that particular counselee.

In giving homework, it's important for you as an effective biblical counselor to be flexible in the homework you've determined to assign your counselee. You need to decide how much you give, and how to use it in the counseling session. You need to make it clear whether this homework is to be shared or if the counselee is to receive the benefit while working on it at home alone. You need to be conscious of how much time he has to devote to the completion of homework. You need to take his reading skills and intellectual abilities under consideration so you don't give him more than he can handle. Your expectations must be tailored to his abilities. If you're not flexible, the homework may prove to be a frustrating detriment instead of a benefit.

Implementation may also be encouraged by giving what could be called "evaluative assignments." These are especially helpful for Inventory, Interpretation and Implementation purposes.

For example, you might ask the person to make a list of ways in which he has made progress and a list of problems on which he has made little or no progress. Find out what *he* thinks. Your counselee is evaluating himself while you're evaluating him.

Another example is having him list all of the fifteen characteristics of true love, biblical love (found in 1 Cor. 13:4-8). Have him define each characteristic and evaluate himself for each in terms of *Always, Frequently, Sometimes, Seldom,* and *Never.* This is one of my favorite assignments.

Here's another one. I call it a "temptation plan." It helps

the counselee come up with his own gameplan for defeating particular temptations in his life. It's a log or outline to help him when he is tempted. Here is an example of a temptation plan. In such a plan, your counselees should:

- Pay attention to times and places when they recognize and acknowledge they are being tempted (1 Cor. 10:13);
- Pray (Ps. 50:15);
- If possible, remove themselves from the occasion or place of temptation (Gen. 39:12);
- Identify the unbiblical desires they are struggling with at this point (1 John 2:15-16);
- Think of or recite verses such as Philippians 4:8, Ephesians 4:22-24 and Romans 12:1-2;
- Remind themselves of the serious consequences of yielding and of the benefits of godly obedience (1 Cor. 6:18-20);
- Remember their commitment to do the godly thing when faced with temptation;
- Repeat this process until the power of the temptation is alleviated;
- If they feel especially vulnerable or weak, they are to call a supportive friend and ask for help (Gal. 6:1-3).

Many times, such a plan as this allows your counselees to rightly respond to temptation. But what happens if they don't? Do we drop their case and move on to the next one? Or do we provide help and assistance even when they fail?

Yes, you guessed it. There should be a "recovery plan." As you explain it to your counselee, it might go something like this:

If I fail to respond rightly to temptation, I will:

- Immediately put biblical repentance into action. I will call what I have done what God calls it—sin. I will confess this sin to God, and take full responsibility for it. I will reflect on the awfulness of sin and the awfulness of the way it makes me feel inside. I will be concerned about my heart sins as much as my behavioral ones. I will turn to Christ and reflect on 1 John 1:9. I will ask God for forgiveness and help and remind myself of God's promise of forgiveness (Eph. 1:7).

- I will examine and identify what I did that I shouldn't have done and what I should have done.
- I will acknowledge my sin to the person or persons to whom I have made myself accountable.
- I will purpose to forget the past (Phil. 3:13) and press onward. I will get back up and start again (Prov. 24:16).
- If there is someone to whom I must make restitution, I will do whatever is fitting and possible.
- I will review my temptation plan and recommit myself to putting it into practice the next time I'm tempted.

As with the other elements of effective biblical counseling, Implementation is hard. It requires thought and time. But without it, any encouragement for change is only academic. Implementation is practical. It is a way to show the hurting person how to take positive steps toward change.

Sometimes our counselees make great strides and cause us to praise God for intervening so quickly in their lives. Sometimes it seems they're taking baby steps—and that's fine as long as there is progress.

The next and final step in promoting true biblical change is *Integration*, where it all comes together. I pray you're as excited about learning this crucial step as I am about teaching it.

Extended book list for
homework recommendations

Books by Wayne Mack	Books by Other Authors
A Christian Growth and Discipleship Manual—Wayne Mack	ADHD—Edward T. Welch
A Fight to the Death—Wayne Mack and Joshua Mack	Age of Opportunity—Paul David Tripp
A Homework Manual for Biblical Living, Volume 1 and 2—Wayne Mack	Get Outta My Face!—Rick Horne
Anger and Stress Management God's Way—Wayne Mack	Help! I'm So Lonely—Deborah Howard
Down but Not Out—Wayne Mack	Help! Someone I Love has Alzheimer's—Deborah Howard and Judith K. Howe
God's Solutions to Life's Problems—Wayne Mack and Joshua Mack	Help! Someone I Love has Cancer—Deborah Howard
Humility: A Forgotten Virtue—Wayne Mack and Joshua Mack	Homosexuality—Edward T. Welch
In-Laws—Wayne Mack	Knowing God—J. I. Packer
It's Not Fair!—Wayne Mack and Deborah Howard	Marriage, Divorce, and Remarriage—Jay Adams
Life in the Father's House—Wayne Mack and Dave Swavely	Pain—Jim Halla
Maximum Impact—Wayne Mack	Pornography—David Powlison
Out of the Blues—Wayne Mack	Power Encounters—David Powlison
Preparing for Marriage God's Way—Wayne Mack	Saved Without a Doubt—John MacArthur
Reaching the Ear of God—Wayne Mack	Sex, Romance and the Glory of God—C. J. Mahaney
Strengthening Your Marriage—Wayne Mack	Shepherding a Child's Heart—Tedd Tripp

Books by Wayne Mack	Books by Other Authors
Sweethearts for a Lifetime—Wayne Mack	Spiritual Depression: Its Causes and Cure—David Martyn Lloyd-Jones
The Fear Factor—Wayne Mack and Joshua Mack	Sunsets: Reflections for Life's Final Journey—Deborah Howard
The Twin Pillars of the Christian Life—Wayne Mack and Joshua Mack	Teach Them Diligently—Lou Priolo
You Can Overcome Despondency—Wayne Mack	The Gospel for Everyday Life—Jerry Bridges
Your Family God's Way—Wayne Mack	The Heart of Anger—Lou Priolo
	The Pilgrim's Progress—John Bunyan (edited by Cheryl Ford)
	The Practice of Godliness—Jerry Bridges
	The Pursuit of Holiness—Jerry Bridges
	The Quest for More—Paul David Tripp
	Transforming Grace—Jerry Bridges
	Trusting God—Jerry Bridges
	Ultimate Questions—John Blanchard
	War of Words—Paul David Tripp
	What Did You Expect?—Paul David Tripp
	When Sinners Say "I Do"—Dave Harvey
	Where is God in All of This?—Deborah Howard
	You Never Stop Being a Parent—Jim Newheiser

9

Integration

We are finally ready to tackle this last element of the eight "I"s—*Integration*. What do I mean by Integration? It basically means the combining of one thing with another so that they become a whole entity. In the scope of biblical counseling, it means that we want to "integrate" or "combine" the principles of Scripture into our lives and facilitate integration into the lives of those we seek to help.

I hope to accomplish four purposes with this chapter.

1. Explain the various components of Integration.
2. Demonstrate the importance and method of working with the counselee or child or disciple or friend until unbiblical patterns of life have been put off and biblical patterns of life have become habitual.
3. Explain and emphasize that the goal of biblical counseling is the integration of biblical directives into the life of the person, and integration of the person into the life of the church.
4. Give instruction on the when and the how of terminating the counseling relationship.

Basically, two kinds of integration are under discussion here. Scripture makes it crystal clear that biblical principles must be integrated into our lives. How does this happen? By learning God's Word, and being trained to interpret it and apply it to our lives.

This kind of integration is stressed by many passages in the

Bible. Here are but a few:

- "For those who live according to the flesh set their minds on the things of the flesh, but those who live according to the Spirit set their minds on the things of the Spirit. To set the mind on the flesh is death, but to set the mind on the Spirit is life and peace" (Rom. 8:5–6).
- "I appeal to you therefore, brothers, by the mercies of God, to present your bodies as a living sacrifice, holy and acceptable to God, which is your spiritual worship. Do not be conformed to this world, but be transformed by the renewal of your mind, that by testing you may discern what is the will of God, what is good and acceptable and perfect" (Rom. 12:1–2).
- "Rather train yourself for godliness" (1 Tim. 4:7).
- "But solid food is for the mature, for those who have their powers of discernment trained by constant practice to distinguish good from evil" (Heb. 5:14).
- "All Scripture is breathed out by God and profitable for teaching, for reproof, for correction, and for training in righteousness, that the man of God may be competent, equipped for every good work" (2 Tim. 3:16–17; see also Eph. 4:1, Col. 1:9–11).

The second kind of integration is no less important. Scripture also makes it clear that Christians are to be integrated into the church. We are not designed to be loners or hermits. For instance, how can we practice the "one anothers" of Scripture while living on our own? No, we are to have a function in the local church—practicing godliness towards one another.

This kind of integration is stressed by many passages in the Bible. Here are but a few:

- "And day by day, attending the temple together and breaking bread in their homes, they received their food with glad and generous hearts, praising God and having favor with all the people. And the Lord added to their number day by day those who were being saved" (Acts 2:46–47).

- "For as in one body we have many members, and the members do not all have the same function, so we, though many, are one body in Christ, and individually members one of another" (Rom. 12:4–5).
- "Rather, speaking the truth in love, we are to grow up in every way into him who is the head, into Christ, from whom the whole body, joined and held together by every joint with which it is equipped, when each part is working properly, makes the body grow so that it builds itself up in love" (Eph. 4:15–16; see Eph 4:1–16.)
- "Him we proclaim, warning everyone and teaching everyone with all wisdom, that we may present everyone mature in Christ" (Col. 1:28).
- "And let us consider how to stir up one another to love and good works, not neglecting to meet together, as is the habit of some, but encouraging one another and all the more as you see the Day drawing near" (Heb. 10:24–25).

In light of this, we can draw a couple of conclusions. For one thing, if it is God's revealed will for biblical principles to be integrated into our lives, we must know how and why these principles can be integrated. A second conclusion is that since it is God's will for us to be integrated into the life of a local church, we should know how and why that is so.

The passages above illustrated both the "hows" and the "whys" of integrating the truths of Scripture into our lives. The "how" is by learning the Word of God, knowing what pleases our Lord, and what does not. We are to learn by study, by reading, by memorizing, by listening to sound preaching, and by reading good spiritual books. Several passages stress the word "training." We are to be trained for this. It takes effort and practice. It is only when we know God's Word that we can begin to apply it to our lives in obedience to it.

The "why" is also given to us. The main answer is because God tells us we are. He is our Creator, and thus is our final Authority. We do what He tells us to do. And He tells us we are to learn His Word. God receives glory when we are obedient to His Word.

However, we also derive many benefits from our obedience to these scriptural commands and principles. Obedience protects us. Obedience blesses us and brings peace. Obedience to these principles causes us to be more profitable in every endeavor and more successful in every relationship.

Obedience provides the framework for our service to God as well as our worship and praise. It causes us to better reflect the redemption and regeneration He has given us. Our obedience makes us better witnesses of His saving love.

Obedience does not guarantee our lives will be roses and sunshine. In fact, we're told that our lives as Christians will be marked by continued suffering. In such times, how great is the blessing of knowing His Word, so we can apply it to each trial that comes our way. And Christ, our Redeemer, is with us every step of the way—whether the road is rocky or smooth.

The second conclusion is that we are to be integrated into a local church. This is truly a benefit for the hurting ones who come to us for counsel. We don't leave them alone to fend for themselves after our counseling is finished. If they become integrated into a local church, they continue to be taught, nourished, loved, and held accountable. When they become part of a local church, they are accepted immediately into the family of God—with brothers and sisters who can support, comfort, and encourage.

How they do this is easy—they begin attending a local church and put themselves forward for membership. Why are they to do it? I mentioned some of the benefits in the previous paragraph. But again, the main "why" is because God, our Creator, our final Authority, has commanded us to do this. It glorifies Him when we follow Him in obedience.

"Now you are the body of Christ and individually members of it" (1 Cor. 12:27).

"And he put all things under his feet and gave him as head over all things to the church, which is his body, the fullness of him who fills all in all" (Eph. 1:22–23).

"I hope to come to you soon, but I am writing these things

to you so that, if I delay, you may know how one ought to behave in the household of God, which is the church of the living God, a pillar and buttress of truth" (1 Tim. 3:14–15).

In that last verse alone, we see that the church is "the household or family of God." It is also "the church of the living God." It says the church is "a pillar of the truth." As a buttress, it is the support, chair, or defense of the truth.

The church is vitally important to the Triune God. We glorify Him when we belong to His body, the church. And He blesses us through it.

Two little words convince me that every believer should be integrated into a local church. These two words are found fifty-eight times in the last twenty-two books of the Bible, emphasizing eight specific ministries that every Christian should do for others, and should receive from others. These ministries can only be fulfilled in a maximum way within the context of a commitment to a body of people with whom they meet on a regular and consistent basis.

These two little words, as I mentioned earlier, are "one another." These words are used repeatedly to describe the responsibility that can only be fulfilled by the household of God—especially in the local church.

Effective biblical counselors must keep these two words in mind as they counsel. We are to facilitate, as much as possible, the putting off of unbiblical attitudes and behaviors—and the sins that grow from these, and the putting on of biblical attitudes and behaviors—and the blessings that result from these.

What criteria should the biblical counselor use to determine when integration has occurred? What criteria should be used to indicate the conclusion of the counseling process?

The *general* answer: Since the goal of biblical counseling is to integrate biblical principles into the life of the counselee and to integrate the counselee into the life of the church, biblical counselors may terminate counseling when these two aspects of integration have occurred in the person's life.

A *specific* answer: An effective counselor may terminate further counseling when they see these events taking place:

- The counselee understands and interprets problems and solutions biblically;
- The counselee notes a decrease in frequency and intensity of temptation;
- There is the experience of victory where and when the person had previously failed;
- The counselee's failures are understood and handled in a biblical manner;
- The counselee self-evaluates and believes the need for counseling has passed;
- Positive movement is demonstrated on a progress list;
- Positive reports are received from others;
- The counselee becomes a counselor or discipler to someone else and begins to promote the importance of counseling;
- Progress continues as time between sessions is lengthened;
- The counselee becomes more involved in the church, is regularly and beneficially receiving good, theologically sound, practical teaching from the pastors and teachers, and is developing relationships with other godly people.

This leads to the question of how we should end the counseling process. In most cases, this decision is made by the counselor in conjunction with the counselee. You may choose to lengthen the time between sessions as a way to begin. For instance, you may go from seeing the person every two weeks to once a month, to every other month, and finally to every six months.

It should be done in such a way that neither the counselor nor the counselee is convinced that more time is needed. Even when the formal sessions have stopped, the counselee must rest in the knowledge that you are a phone call away should he need to talk. You may even want to schedule a yearly "tune-up" meeting just to make sure the person has remained committed to following the principles of Scripture and is still fully integrated into the body of a local church.

10

Conclusion

A t the beginning of this book, I mentioned several objectives in writing it. Let's revisit them now.

- To provide a biblical foundation for using the Scriptures in dealing with your own spiritual problems and the spiritual problems of others;
- To demonstrate the value of using the Bible, rather than worldly wisdom, to deal with problems;
- To familiarize the reader with the issues that people face and give an accurate paradigm for evaluating them so the necessary assistance can be provided;
- To enlarge compassion and ability to help others make biblical changes and become better disciples of Jesus Christ;
- To provide a procedure to use in dealing with any counseling situation—in your own life as well as the lives of others;
- To challenge the personal and spiritual development necessary to qualify a believer to minister to others.

I went on to clarify that I wrote this book to offer some guidelines and checklists to help you help others become better disciples of Jesus Christ. I wanted to give you the eight "I"s of effective biblical counseling—a methodology I've been honing for many years.

These eight "I"s are biblically based elements for promoting biblical change in yourself or in others. This will help enable you to fulfill certain commands of Scripture. What are some of these commands? Here are a few:

> "Go therefore and *make disciples of all nations,* baptizing them in the name of the Father and of the Son and of the Holy Spirit, *teaching them to observe all that I have commanded you.* And behold, I am with you always, to the end of the age" (Matt. 28:19–20, emphasis added).

> "Rather, speaking the truth in love, we are to grow up in every way into him who is the head, into Christ" (Eph. 4:15).

> "Him we proclaim, warning everyone and teaching everyone with all wisdom, that we may present everyone mature in Christ" (Col. 1:28).

These passages and more instruct us, as believers, to grow in spiritual maturity, to learn the Word of God, to conform to Christ's likeness, and to draw ever closer to the Savior we love and obey. It says more than that. It also says we are to teach others, to guide them in their walk, to present them to Christ, mature and holy.

The Bible is crystal clear in saying that we are to do these things. However, the one prerequisite to doing this ourselves and/or helping others attain a level of spiritual maturity is to *know His Word.* We can't apply it unless we know it. God doesn't mysteriously zap it into our brains. Instead, He wrote this Bible as a love letter to His children. We have the responsibility to study it, and then to learn and grow as a consequence of our study.

This requires time, effort, and perseverance. Yet, truly knowing God's Word is worth any time and effort we put into learning it. It gives us our only glimpse of Almighty God, our Sovereign Creator. It provides knowledge of the most important God-man, Jesus Christ, who secured our salvation by His life, death, and resurrection. It allows us to comprehend truths of the precious Holy Spirit, without whom we could not understand the truths of God's Word.

If we truly belong to God, we will have a thirst to learn more about Him. We don't all have to become biblical scholars, but it behooves us to have a good, working knowledge of the Bible. Not only does it introduce us to our Triune God, but it provides for us all the tools we will ever need to live a life pleasing to Him.

I've found the eight "I"s to be incredibly helpful to me in my own counseling and discipling ministry. I use them as the paradigm I follow in every counseling relationship. I hope you will find them as helpful as I have, and that you will use them faithfully as a guide for your own ministry as well.

At the beginning of the book, I gave you definitions of the eight "I"s. In the body of the book, I told you that progress reports were helpful in assessing the success or failure of the sessions. So, I'd like to offer those definitions again. Now that you've read the entire book, these eight "I"s should be like old friends instead of strangers, as they were in the beginning.

Read them again. I think you'll see how much progress you've made just by reading through each chapter. Now you're familiar with them, and I hope you'll refer to them over and over.

Definitions of these eight key elements of biblical change—the eight "I"s—are as follow:

1. *Involvement:* Promotes biblical change by establishing a change-facilitating relationship.
2. *Inspiration:* According to Webster's dictionary, inspiration involves influencing, stimulating, arousing or producing a thought or feeling. In this case, in promoting biblical change, we want to inspire, arouse, or influence the counsel-ee to develop and sustain an attitude and feeling of hope that will promote biblical change.
3. *Inventory/Investigation:* Promotes biblical change by securing enough of the right kinds of information so that we can accurately understand the counselee and his problems.
4. *Interpretation:* Promotes biblical change by analyzing and organizing the information we have gathered so we can accurately identify the biblical nature and cause or causes of the counselee's problems, then convincingly explain them.
5. *Instruction:* Promotes biblical change by giving accurate, appropriate, and relevant biblical instruction that provides God's perspective on what to do to solve the problems.

6. *Inducement:* Promotes biblical change by encouraging (inducing persuading) the counselee to repent of sinful attitudes, words, and actions and make a decisive commitment to obey the Lord and follow biblical directives.

7. *Implementation:* Promotes biblical change by helping the counselee plan how to make the biblical directives a reality in his life.

8. *Integration:* Promotes biblical change by coaching and mentoring the counselee until the necessary changes are integrated into his life, encouraging integration into the life of the church.

I hope the suggestions and illustrations I've provided will help you in your own ministry to help hurting people. Some readers may have been confused or intimidated about counseling others. If you are one of them, I hope you are less intimidated now and will continue to learn and grow in knowledge, experience, and ability.

This teaching encapsulates the scope of my counseling experience over the years. I've personally seen thousands find true biblical change through these elements. May God richly bless you as you endeavor to glorify Christ and nurture one another in Him.

About Shepherd Press Publications

They are gospel driven.
They are heart focused.
They are life changing.

Our Invitation to You

We passionately believe that what we are publishing can be of benefit to you, your family, your friends, and your work colleagues. So we are inviting you to join our online mailing list so that we may reach out to you with news about our latest and forthcoming publications, and with special offers.

Visit:

www.shepherdpress.com/newsletter

and provide your name and email address.

COUNSEL FOR THE HEART

A RESOURCE for WORD-BASED
TRANSFORMATION and
PRACTICAL DISCIPLESHIP